For John & Stephanie,

  The South, although, alas not the USSR, will rise again!

Gene

The Slaveholders' Dilemma

The Jack N. and Addie D. Averitt Lecture Series, 1990
Delivered at Georgia Southern University
Statesboro, Georgia

The Slaveholders' Dilemma

Freedom and Progress in Southern Conservative Thought, 1820–1860

EUGENE D. GENOVESE

University of South Carolina Press

Published in Columbia, South Carolina, by the
University of South Carolina Press

Manufactured in Canada.

Library of Congress Cataloging-in-Publication Data

Genovese, Eugene D., 1930–
    The slaveholders' dilemma : freedom and progress in southern
conservative thought, 1820–1860 / Eugene D. Genovese.
        p.   cm.
    "The Jack N. and Addie D. Averitt lecture series, 1990; delivered
at Georgia Southern University."
    Includes bibliographical references and index.
    ISBN 0–87249–783–6 (hardcover : acid-free)
    1. Slavery — Southern States — Justification.   2. Slaveholders —
Southern States — Intellectual life.   3. Southern States —
Intellectual life.   I. Title.   II. Title: Jack N. and Addie D.
Averitt lecture series.
E449.G3725   1991
306.3'62'0975 — dc20   91-26735

For

M. E. Bradford,
John Shelton Reed,
Clyde N. Wilson,

scholars, gentlemen, worthy heirs of a
great Southern Tradition

And Abram went up out of Egypt, he and his wife, and all that he had, and Lot with him, into the South. . . .

And the land was not able to bear them, that they might dwell together: for their substance was great, so that they could not dwell together. . . .

And Abram said unto Lot, Let there be no strife, I pray thee, between me and thee, and between my herdmen and thy herdmen; for we *be* brethren. . . .

Then Lot chose him all the plain of Jordan; and Lot journeyed east: and they separated themselves the one from the other.

Abram dwelled in the land of Canaan, and Lot dwelled in the cities of the plain, and pitched *his* tent toward Sodom.

Genesis 13: 1–12

Contents

Foreword

University Week on the campus of Georgia Southern University, October 8–13, 1990, marked the celebration of long-sought university status and the inauguration of the Jack N. and Addie D. Averitt Lecture Series. Both events represented milestones in the academic life of the eighty-four-year-old institution. Endowed by Graduate Dean Emeritus and Mrs. Averitt, the lectureship was a gift to the History and English Departments to provide annual lectures by leading scholars in the respective disciplines. The series was designed to enhance on-campus academic and cultural life for students, faculty, and community.

Professor Averitt, a native of Statesboro, Georgia, has had a lifelong relationship with Georgia Southern. After receiving his undergraduate degree at then Georgia Teachers College, he earned the M.A. at the University of Georgia and his Ph.D. at the University of North Carolina. While at Chapel Hill, Professor Averitt was named a Fulbright Fellow and served as a visiting lecturer at King's College, University of London. Having begun his college teaching career at Georgia Teachers College prior to his doctoral studies, Professor Averitt returned to his alma mater where he later became chairman of the Social Science Division. In 1968 he was appointed dean of the graduate school, a position he held until his retirement in 1979. Besides his distinguished career as a scholar, teacher, and educator, Professor Averitt has been a successful real estate developer and civic leader. A modern Renaissance man, his talents range from music to architecture.

In 1946 Addie Dunnaway joined the staff at Georgia Teachers College as a reference librarian. A native of Clarksville, Tennessee, she graduated from Peabody College and earned a graduate degree in library science from Vanderbilt-Peabody. The Averitts were married in 1948. Accompanying her husband to Chapel Hill in 1950, Mrs. Averitt served as Director of Elementary School Library Programs, Durham City Schools, Durham, North Carolina, until 1954.

Professor and Mrs. Averitt have received international recognition for their selfless contributions to both Rotary Foundation and Rotary International. For nine years Professor Averitt directed the Rotary Foundation Summer Language Institute at Georgia Southern, which attracted two hundred international scholars to campus annually for ten weeks of intensive study of English as a second language. Under his leadership, the Georgia Southern Institute subsequently became the model for similar programs in France and Japan. Nearly two thousand students from fifty-two countries ultimately came to Georgia Southern, making it one of the best known institutions of higher education in the world.

In recognition for distinguished service to Rotary, Professor Averitt has received many honors, including Harris Fellow, Rotary International; Distinguished Service Award, Rotary Foundation; Man of the Year Statesboro and Bulloch County; Trustee of the Rotary Foundation; and District Governor of Rotary International. Mrs. Averitt holds the unique honor of being the first woman to receive Rotary Foundation's Distinguished Service Award.

Professor Averitt, Dean Emeritus of the Graduate School and Professor Emeritus of History, has been associated with Georgia Southern University in various capacities for six decades. He has seen the institution grow from normal school to become the state's newest university. As graduate dean and director of the Rotary Language Institute, he has touched the lives of students from around the globe. Through the establishment of this lecture series, Professor and Mrs. Averitt reaffirm their commitment to academic excellence and the future of Georgia Southern University.

Many individuals share the credit for the success of the first Averitt lectures. The lecture committee was indeed fortunate to engage Professor Eugene D. Genovese to open the series. True to his reputation as one of the premier historians of the American South, Professor Genovese set a superlative standard for those who will follow. These lectures will no doubt be received as a major contribution to the historiography of southern intellectual history. Thanks are due to Marilyn Bruce who coordinated University Week events; to Professor Walter J. Fraser, Jr., Chair, Department of History, who kept us on track; and, most especially, I am grateful to my colleagues Fred Brogdon, Esther Mallard, Anastatia Sims, and George Shriver who served faithfully and regularly on the lecture series committee. Mrs. Mallard, ever the gracious hostess, insisted that the traditions of southern hospitality remain inviolate. Finally, we are indebted to Warren Slesinger of the University of South Carolina Press, who was enthusiastic about this endeavor from the outset and who has guided the lectures into print.

R. FRANK SAUNDERS, JR.
Professor and Chairman
Averitt Lecture Committee

Georgia Southern University
Statesboro, Georgia
January 1991

Preface

To have been invited to inaugurate the Averitt Lecture Series at
Georgia Southern University and thereby also to participate in
the celebration of the establishment of my adopted state's newest
institution of higher learning was a singular honor that I shall
always cherish. I am indebted to the administrators, faculty, and
students of Georgia Southern and to the people of Statesboro for
their challenging responses, which, I trust, have enabled me to
improve this somewhat expanded version of the lectures.

My wife and I were deeply touched by the reception we were
accorded by Dr. and Mrs. Jack Averitt, Mr. and Mrs. Jack Mallard,
and the members of the Georgia Southern community. Professor
R. F. Saunders, Jr., Chairman of the Averitt Lecture Committee,
proved an exemplary host, and I felt especially favored by a gracious and, for me, memorable introduction to the first lecture by
an old friend, Professor Emerita Julia F. Smith. All in all, it should
be enough to say that my wife and I were treated in accordance
with the highest standards of southern hospitality.

Several friends read the manuscript and offered salutary crit-
icisms and suggestions: Carol Bleser, Stanley L. Engerman, Drew
Gilpin Faust, Lou Ferleger, David Moltke-Hansen, and Robert
L. Paquette. I am especially indebted to Professor Moltke-
Hansen for his critical reading of the discussion of William Hen-

ry Trescot, a subject on which he has unparalleled expertise. Similarly, I am indebted to Professors Bleser and Faust for their expert readings of the discussion of James Henry Hammond, the more so since I have advanced an interpretation that simultaneously builds on their excellent work while departing from it in one essential respect.

John Merriman took time away from writing his doctoral dissertation at Emory University to assist in the compilation of materials and the checking of references and, as he often does, to offer his valuable insights into southern history.

Elizabeth Fox-Genovese, in addition to performing her customary wifely duties as critic and editor, was kind enough to allow me to draw freely upon the work we have been doing together for many years for our book-in-progress, *The Mind of the Master Class: The Life and Thought of the Southern Slaveholders*. These lectures are, in a sense, an introduction to a few of the themes we shall be pursuing at length in that book.

Part of the work on that book and this one was done at the National Humanities Center in North Carolina during the two years I was privileged to spend there as a Fellow, and it is a pleasure to acknowledge the assistance provided by its superb staff, as well as by Drs. Carolyn Wallace, Richard Shrader, and the late Mattie Russell at the manuscript collections of the nearby University of North Carolina and Duke University. Indeed, as always for southern historians, it is a pleasure to express gratitude to the staffs at the University of South Carolina and other libraries and state archives, whose unfailing courtesy and skill proved indispensable.

The text contains some shorthand that I would have preferred to avoid. The very terms "progress," "freedom," and even "slavery" remain ambiguous, but I have done my best along the way to delineate the meanings appropriate to the specific subject matter. More troubling, I decided to risk the invocation of other imprecise and ambiguous terms rather than burden the text with interminable and, in the end, probably unenlightening elaborations of meanings and nuances. I have, that is, assumed that the terms convey significant meanings with the minimal clarity necessary for the argument. Thus, "modernity," the several meanings of which would take a volume to explore, stands for the growing tendency to place the individual at the center of art as well as social life. The wretched word "modernization," which means different things to sociologists and economists and to those of different ideologies, stands as a loose but suggestive expression for industrialization and political and social democratization, with all their inherently contradictory tendencies and meanings.

Especially clumsy are the references to "traditional conservatives" and "bourgeois conservatives." Whether in the South or in Europe, these categories rarely if ever appeared in pure form and are invoked to indicate primary tendencies among those who often swayed back and forth over time and in response to particular problems. The term "traditional conservatives" refers to those who rejected capitalism, the free market, and bourgeois social relations, notwithstanding the frequent concessions they had to make in politics and ideology. The term "bourgeois conservatives" refers to those who reacted against the political, social, and cultural exigencies of industrial capitalism and who tried to defend "traditional values" while they nonetheless accepted, often enthusiastically, the prevailing system of bourgeois social relations. A full treatment of the intellectual and ideological currents of the day would have to pay careful attention to the nuances and changes over time. Here, the terms invoked, however crude, may serve as an adequate first approximation toward the explanation of the limited point this book tries to make about the slaveholders' view of the relation of freedom to progress.

Professor Faust has suggested that in chapter one I may seem to imply a static view that takes no account of the shift in thinking from decade to decade. For example, the economic depression that followed the panic of 1837 and lasted well into the 1840s undoubtedly strengthened southern doubts about the reality of progress and led to enhanced concern with the perceived moral decline that seemed responsible for the sudden decline in material life. Again, I have no doubt that a careful delineation of such trends, which would be appropriate for a big book, would introduce interesting qualifications into my principal argument. But for the limited purposes of this brief essay, such qualifications would threaten the argument itself only if it were unsound in the first place. I must therefore trust serious readers — the only readers who concern me — to provide their own discounts along the way while they make allowance for the weaknesses inevitable in a small book on a big subject.

Atlanta, Georgia
October 1990

The Slaveholders' Dilemma

Introduction

These lectures were intended primarily as a contribution to intellectual history. The first question that might arise would therefore concern resonance. Did the intellectuals discussed here have much influence? Did they, as it were, speak for their people, in particular for the slaveholders? The answer to both questions is yes. To defend the answer would require a leisurely book that closely examined the relation of southern intellectual life to society and institutions in political context. These lectures are a small slice of such a book, which Elizabeth Fox-Genovese and I have been working on for the last fifteen years or so and hope to have ready before too many more years go by.

If the claim of influence and resonance cannot possibly be defended here, one hint may encourage skeptics to suspend disbelief. The southern intellectuals under discussion and the much larger number who shared their views controlled the educational system of the Old South from top to bottom. The power of the Presbyterian divines, for example, would be hard to exaggerate. And the South had proportionately more of its youth in college than the North did.

The slaveholders were a well-educated class by the standards of nineteenth-century America and by those of much of Europe as well. Their religious, political, and social leaders were intellectually impressive and stood up well in comparison with their northern counterparts. The problem of their relation to the yeomanry occasions heated debates among able historians who read the same evidence differently. That problem must be bypassed here. But surely, no one could reasonably argue that the worldview of the slaveholders could be treated lightly without doing violence to the historical record, whatever judgment may be rendered on its extension to other classes.

Many American intellectual historians may cavil at a book that takes the southern intellectuals seriously, not merely as a political force but as people who matched their northern counterparts in learning and creativity. The Emersons, Adamses, and other New Englanders, who demonstrably knew little about southern intellectual life, announced that southerners had no minds, only temperaments. American intellectual historians have been peddling that bigoted nonsense ever since without, I very much fear, bothering to read the appropriate texts. Let us set aside the special problem of northern preeminence in the writing of novels, although the southern performance might look a great deal better if we would condescend to consider such women novelists as Augusta Jane Evans along with the men.[1] On one subject after another the intellectuals of the Old South matched and in some cases overmatched the best the North had to offer.

St. George Tucker, T. R. R. Cobb, Thomas Ruffin in legal theory and jurisprudence; George Tucker and Jacob N. Cardozo in political economy; James Henley Thornwell and Robert L. Dabney in theology and ecclesiology; Thomas Roderick Dew and William H. Trescot in historical studies; John C. Calhoun and Albert Taylor Bledsoe in political theory — the list could be extended — deserve to rank among America's ablest thinkers. (Who now remembers that the luminaries of New England hailed Trescot's *Diplomacy of the Revolution* as America's first great contribution to diplomatic history?) But most of these southerners defended slavery, and even St. George Tucker and George Tucker, who did not, staunchly defended "southern rights" and the political principles and policies of the slaveholders' regime. The slaveholders lost the war; slavery has properly been condemned as an enormity; and, not surprisingly, the southern intellectuals have virtually been expunged from memory.

The loss is ours on two counts. First, the stubborn refusal of most American historians to take seriously the intellectual life of the Old South has gravely weakened our ability to assess the strength of the proslavery cause and account for its depth throughout the South. And even today, it gravely weakens our ability to assess the persistent political and intellectual power of a southern conservatism that participates in a "Reaganite" coalition dominated by the very kind of free-marketeers it has always detested. For in truth, the proslavery argument was by no means merely the shabby rationale of an oppressive social order that it has usually been made out to be. To be sure, at its worst it was just that. But at its formidable best it was also the pillar of a worldview buttressed by close considerations of the great social, political, religious, economic, and philosophical issues of the day.

Second, we could, if we would, profit greatly from a reasoned engagement with the thought of Calhoun, Dew, Bledsoe, Thornwell, and others as we grapple today with the staggering problems of a world in headlong transition to the Lord knows what. The finest aspects of their thought, shorn of the tragic commitment to slavery and racism, constitute a searing critique of some of the most dangerous tendencies in modern life. That subject, however, will have to be left for a more appropriate time and place.[2]

Here we confront one problem: the slaveholders' ambivalent attitude toward "progress," which revealed much about their worldview and their view of themselves. Common sense dictates that a book on views of progress begin with a definition. Alas, as with many of the dictates of common sense, the demand is easier to make than to satisfy. Each definition of progress put forth in a large literature on the subject runs into substantial challenges, which a much larger book than this would be required to review. Still, no apology need be made for a decision to stay clear of the philosophical quagmire. The issue here concerns the meaning attributed to progress by the slaveholders, and even the most sophisticated of them chose not to define it too closely.

Southern intellectuals distinguished moral from material progress. As Christians, they, like their more religiously conservative northern counterparts, accepted the idea of moral progress only in a quantitative sense. That is, no qualitative advance in morals could be made over the teachings of Jesus Christ, but more and more people were being brought to an acceptance of those teachings, in no small part through the revolutionary material progress in transportation and communications that was being effected by the Christian nations of the West. As for material progress, southerners noted the astonishing transformation of modern times — the industrial revolution and all its works — and they pronounced it self-generating, irreversible, and on the whole good. That transformation in material life, together with the spread of Christianity across the globe and the emergence of republican institutions and individual freedom for unprecedented numbers of men, combined to create a magnificent new epoch in human history. Southern intellectuals, like others, called it "progress" and embraced it as their own cause. Simultaneously, they found in it much to hate and fear.

History, ancient and medieval as well as American, fascinated educated southerners. They learned a good deal in school, although much of it in courses in moral philosophy, the Greek and Roman classics, constitutional and municipal law, and other subjects. The slaveholders' diaries, letters, and other personal papers show that the Bible and religious tracts held pride of place in their reading, with history, political tracts, and English literature, most notably Shakespeare, in competition for runner-up. In the academies and colleges students got large doses of Greek and Roman history as well as literature, and many retained a lifelong interest, although few had learned the languages well enough to continue to read in the original. No doubt they had many reasons for their continued interest, including and perhaps especially sheer pleasure. Among those reasons was the moral and historical support they found for their adherence to a slave society. The proslavery theorists never tired of proclaiming that the greatness of ancient Egypt, Israel, Greece, and Rome had been based on slavery, and the reading of ancient history and literature seemed to confirm the proclamation.

Educated southerners did not assume an uncritical stance toward the ancient world. In particular, southern educators, ministers, and legal scholars denounced early Roman patriarchalism for giving the male head of household despotic power over women, children, and slaves.[3] According to the generally held interpretation, which, so far as I know, no southern writer of note contradicted, legal reforms and especially Christianity rescued the ancient world from the evils of despotic patriarchalism and opened the way to a genuinely humane and civilized life. The impetus to the ancient world's progress in morals and social relations thus emerged as the slow development of a rule of law increasingly influenced by the spirit of Christianity. In the prevailing southern view, as virtually every antiabolitionist polemic makes clear, the South stood as the heir and guardian of that great Western tradition, and "Christian slavery" stood as the modern bastion against a relapse into barbarism.

The slaveholders displayed a conflicted attitude toward historical progress, which surfaced from time to time in their considerations of ancient history and burst forth in their considerations of medieval.[4] They did not identify their society with that of the Middle Ages and certainly did not identify themselves as other than modern men who gloried in the material, artistic, and political advances of the nineteenth century. They understood the difference between seigneurialism and slavery, medieval lords and modern slaveholders, serfs and slaves, manors and plantations, feudalism and republicanism. They interpreted the Middle Ages in a manner complex, nuanced, and on the whole well balanced.

As Protestants, the slaveholders scorned the Middle Ages for wallowing in superstition, idolatry, and corrupted religious values — in short, for wallowing in Roman Catholicism. Yet they proved surprisingly generous in the tribute they paid to the Catholic Church as a force for social stability. As proudly modern men, they had contempt for medieval economic stagnation and social backwardness. They reacted with disgust to the despotism, violence, ignorance, and lack of amenities. They sharply denounced political interference in the economy as the primary fetter upon social progress. No important southern intellectual, not even George Frederick Holmes, held up the Middle Ages as a model for the modern world or slipped into more than momentary nostalgia.

Yet they recognized much of value in medieval society. They found the roots of modern republicanism in the evolution of feudal institutions and constitutionalism. They warmly praised the emergence of chivalry and the growth of Christian sentiment, however perverted by a Roman Catholic Church they viewed as increasingly corrupt. Mostly, they valued the organic social relations that were overthrown by the triumph of the bourgeoisie and the cash-nexus. A noticeable tension developed in southern thought. On the one hand, the great majority of the educators, theorists, and public men accepted Manchesterian political economy and praised the emergence of economic freedom, which they identified as the *sine qua non* of the wonderful and ever-spiraling material progress of the modern world. On the other hand, drawing upon their study of political economy as well as history, they repeatedly condemned the severing of the lord-serf relation and the withdrawal of support and protection from the laboring masses. One after another, southern educators and theorists charged that the bourgeoisie, driven by greed and a temperament worthy of infidels, had thrown the masses into an economic jungle and left them to an animal existence of privation, brutal exploitation, outright starvation, and hopelessness.

In the end, the slaveholding intellectuals criticized the Middle Ages for backwardness and welcomed the progress that accompanied their passing. But they deeply regretted the price and especially the destruction of the old social ties between rulers and ruled. Hence, while turning away from the Middle Ages and identifying themselves with modernity, they made two related claims for the South as the legitimate heir to the healthy and constructive elements in medieval life.[5] First, the South remained a Christian society, properly reformed in the Protestant sense, and stood as a bastion against the infidelity and heresies of the bourgeois perversion of modernity, which had badly flawed the Enlightenment and brought forth the horrors of the French Revolution, the Terror, political radicalism, and growing social disorder. Second, the South, with its masters and slaves, boasted organic social relations adjusted to a dynamic and progressive modern world. The South, virtually alone, stood for progress and modernity without the terrible evils that plagued the bourgeois societies. It was erecting not some refurbished medievalism, with the social stagnation it implied, but a modern and progressive slave society that rested upon time-honored social and spiritual foundations. Thus southern theorists generally agreed that the progress of some required the progress of all, but they assumed that genuine progress would have to proceed within a stratified order that dispensed rewards unequally.

The contradictions in the slaveholders' interpretation of history and indeed in their self-image seem apparent now but were rarely noticed then. Even their northern adversaries, who might have pummeled them badly on these matters, usually forfeited the chance by settling for charges of hypocrisy and irrationality, when they bothered to notice at all. The economic freedom that feudalism had stifled and that propelled the extraordinary progress of the modern age could hardly be separated historically or analytically from the extension of freedom to the laboring classes — to that emancipation of the serfs the southerners harshly criticized. The southern intellectuals knew that the extension of freedom and the demise of personal servitude held the secret of the progress and modernity they claimed to represent. They invoked the racial argument: Europeans constituted a superior race fit for freedom after a suitable period of Christian tutelage. But, unable to sustain their larger argument on racial grounds, they repeatedly returned to the emancipation of the serfs as the primary cause of the social crisis that threatened to wreck the modern world and plunge it back toward barbarism.

The slaveholders never came to terms with the ambiguity of their interpretation of the Middle Ages or with the ambivalence toward historical progress that it exposed. They tried. But the ambiguity and ambivalence arose again and again in their critique of the modern bourgeois societies and in their defense of slavery. They earnestly sought to champion a modernity purged of distortions and heresy and to present themselves as the carriers of a well-ordered progress in human affairs. In this respect they shared much with transatlantic conservatives of many types. But in bravely meeting the challenge to assess the role of freedom in history, they struck out on a path of their own. At the end of that path they encountered an unforeseen dilemma and a Hobson's choice between grim political alternatives.

NOTES

1. Literary critics and historians have debated the reasons for the weaknesses of the antebellum southern novel and have contributed much toward the clarification of the central issues. Of special importance is the work of Lewis P. Simpson, esp. *The Dispossessed Garden: Pastoral and History in Southern Literature* (Athens: University of Georgia Press, 1975). For a different view see the work of Louis D. Rubin, Jr., esp. *The Edge of the Swamp: A Study in the Literature and Society of the Old South* (Baton Rouge: Louisiana State University Press, 1989). For appraisals of the work of Simpson and Rubin from the viewpoint advanced in this book see: Elizabeth Fox-Genovese and Eugene D. Genovese, "The Cultural History of Southern Slave Society: Reflections on the Work of Lewis P. Simpson," in J. Gerald Kennedy and Daniel Mark Fogel, eds., *American Letters and the Historical Consciousness: Essays in Honor of Lewis P. Simpson* (Baton Rouge: Louisiana State University Press, 1987), pp. 15–41; and Elizabeth Fox-Genovese, "The Fettered Mind: Time, Place, and the Literary Imagination of the Old South," *Georgia Historical Quarterly*, 76 (1990), 622–650.

2. For some suggestions in support of this assertion see my contribution to the symposium on the 1980s in *Commentary*, 90 (1990), 48–50; and my "Critical Legal Studies as Radical Politics and Ideology," *Yale Journal of Law & the Humanities*, 3 (1991), 131–156.

3. Thomas Roderick Dew, who will be discussed in chapter one, stressed this point throughout his work. Every noteworthy writer of whom I am aware took the same position. I know of none who supported the early Roman patriarchy. Rather, the model invoked was that of the Abramic household, which made the patriarch subject to the laws of God and therefore recognized the human rights of wives, children, and dependents.

4. For an elaboration see Eugene D. Genovese, "The Southern Slaveholders' View of the Middle Ages," in Bernard Rosenthal and Paul E. Szarmach, eds., *Medievalism in American Culture: Papers of the Eighteenth Annual Conference of the Center for Medieval and Early Renaissance Studies* (Binghamton, New York: Medieval and Renaissance Texts and Studies, 1989), pp. 31–52.

5. For an especially bold and challenging attempt to subsume southern pro-slavery thought in transatlantic conservatism see Larry E. Tise, *Proslavery: A History of the Defense of Slavery in America, 1701–1840* (Athens: University of Georgia Press, 1987). For a critique see Eugene D. Genovese, "Larry Tise's *Proslavery:* An Appreciation and a Critique," *Georgia Historical Quarterly,* 72 (1988), 670–683. For an especially thoughtful discussion of these and other questions at issue here see James Oakes, *Slavery and Freedom: An Interpretation of the Old South* (New York: Knopf, 1990).

1

The Dilemma

The mainstream of modern Western thought has cast slavery and progress as irreconcilable opposites, insisting that slavery impeded progress by restricting the freedom of every individual to contribute to society through the pursuit of self interest. Slavery, if we are to credit its adversaries, threatened the very identity of the American republic, corroding its virtue and retarding its development. Even the growing demand for rapid economic development through a program of free soil, free labor, and free men elided moral and material progress, tying the fate of the one to the unfolding of the other. The War for Southern Independence appeared to confirm this reading and to embody the triumph of moral and material progress over the forces of stagnation and reaction.

The war, in sealing the triumph of the North over the South, also sealed the triumph of the association of freedom and progress over an alternate reading. If the seeds of the irreconcilable opposition between slavery and progress, like the seeds of the unquestioning association of progress with freedom, were sown in the American, French, and Haitian Revolutions, their blossoming was not immediately assured. The slaveholding intellectuals, clerical and lay, took radically different ground, arguing for an

understanding of freedom and progress as grounded in — not opposed to — slavery as a social system.

Edmund Morgan has demonstrated that the slaveholders of
colonial Virginia espoused slavery as the necessary foundation of
individual freedom and republican virtue and saw themselves as
the principal champions of both. David Brion Davis has demonstrated that important strands of Euro-American thought came to
challenge the prevalent notion that slavery impeded progress and
to conclude that, under certain conditions, slavery in fact generated progress. Despite the inestimable contributions of these and
other learned historians, the southern slaveholders' discrete understanding of the precise interrelation of slavery, freedom, and
progress remains to be explored.[1]

The southern intellectuals devoted a large number of books,
pamphlets, and articles in lay and religious journals to these subjects. The answer they offered, notwithstanding variations of considerable political importance, contained a big surprise. For they
viewed freedom, not slavery, as the driving force in human progress, moral and material. They based their defense of slavery on
a prior defense of freedom, which they identified as the dynamic
in a world progress the cause of which they claimed as their own.
Freedom, in their view, could not be extended to all, but it could
be extended to increasing numbers and could be expected to
result in a better life for those who remained subservient. They
thereby invoked slavery as a positive force that grounded the
social order required to support the freedom necessary for progress. The slaveholders presented themselves to themselves and
to the world as the most reliable carriers of the cause of progress
in Western civilization, and they presented their social system as
the surest and safest model for a worldwide Christendom that
sought to continue its forward march.

The slaveholders had no greater success than others, before
or since, in defining "progress," but they settled, as most others
have, for a common-sense notion of a steady and irreversible
advance in the material conditions of life for the masses as well as

for the elites. However qualified their recognition of moral progress, the slaveholders displayed deep ambivalence toward that material progress which the overwhelming majority of them saw as inevitable: Literally, they loved and hated it. They embraced it on balance partly because they did see it as inevitable, and partly because they welcomed the leisure, knowledge, and comfort it brought. Like most traditionalist conservatives in Europe, they wanted to guide and temper social change, to slow it down so as to avoid destructive effects. Unlike the traditionalist conservatives in Europe, they thought they had found the means in the organization of social relations on a slaveholding basis.

In the eyes of foreign critics, by no means all or even most of whom were abolitionists, the slaveholders of the Old South qualified as reactionaries who were desperately clinging to a retrogressive social system in an age of accelerating economic, social, and intellectual development. Northerners, Britons, continental Europeans, and Latin Americans shook their heads at the existence of a backward yet politically powerful regional regime embedded in an economically dynamic, politically radical — by the standards of the day — republic poised to challenge for world power. The long list of such critics included not only radicals, democrats, and liberals of all stripes, but many high Tories, high churchmen, and other conservatives who shared the slaveholders' grave reservations about the vast changes that were occurring in the wake of the industrial and French revolutions.[2]

Many of these conservatives, to one extent or another, carried into the nineteenth century the attitudes associated with, say, Samuel Johnson during the eighteenth. Even most of those who expressed sympathy for the Confederacy did so because they hated the bourgeois radicalism of the North, valued the conservatism and aristocratic tone of the South, and considered the race question intractable, not because they supported slavery in principle. More often than not — the Vatican may serve as an example — they hoped that the South would find a way to shed slavery and thereby rid itself of a moral incubus and the principal encumbrance to the material well-being required to sustain national independence.

The slaveholders saw themselves differently. Southern intellectuals, political leaders, and ordinary slaveholders, as their numerous diaries and personal papers attest, regarded themselves as progressive men and as active participants in the material and moral march of history. They saw themselves as men who sought an alternate route to modernity.[3] An occasional George Fitzhugh could pronounce himself a reactionary and proclaim, "We want no new world." But then, in our own century, from Allen Tate to M. E. Bradford, the best minds who have contributed to an intellectually powerful southern conservative tradition have teasingly also pronounced themselves reactionaries and yet honestly denied any wish to restore some ancient or medieval regime.[4] It should be enough to recall the significant contributions of Tate, John Crowe Ransom, and their fellow Agrarians to the modernist movement in literary criticism. These modern southern conservatives, like Fitzhugh and the intellectuals of the Old South, have repudiated neither "progress," nor "science," nor "modernity." They have repudiated the cult of progress, scientism, and the moral and political decadence of a modernity run wild.

The dilemma inherent in the slaveholders' contradictory ideas of progress, freedom, and slavery emerges most clearly in the work of Thomas Roderick Dew of Virginia (1802–1846), whose remarkable literary output ranged well beyond his famous review of the debates in the Virginia legislature over emancipation. As president of the College of William and Mary and a professor of history, political economy, moral philosophy, and other subjects, he devoted much of his career to an interpretation of the development of Western civilization. In 1852 a superb exposition of his thought appeared posthumously as *A Digest of the Laws, Customs, Manners and Institutions of the Ancient and Modern Nations*, which even today deserves careful study for its intrinsic value and not merely as a document of southern intellectual history. It may be doubted that his review of the Virginia debates, which constituted a turning point in the proslavery debate, could be fully understood outside the context of the *Digest*, which itself needs to be supplemented by his *Lectures on the Restrictive System* (1829), an able exposition of classical political economy, and his essays on women in history, usury laws, ancient and modern eloquence, and sundry other subjects.[5]

And let it be noted that the *Digest* and the *Restrictive System* consisted, no doubt with some elaboration, of the lectures he delivered to southern youth many of whom went on to positions of leadership in their society. Indeed, some of the most important books of the day grew out of college lectures that had an inestimable influence on the minds of those who would lead southern slave society: Nathaniel Beverley Tucker on political science; George Tucker on political economy; St. George Tucker and Henry St. George Tucker on constitutional law; R. H. Rivers and William A. Smith on moral philosophy; Samuel Henry Dickson on medicine; James Henley Thornwell on theology, ecclesiology, and social theory. That most of these and other authors of college texts expounded a coherent and distinctly proslavery worldview reveals much about the intellectual formation of the youth of the southern elite.[6]

Dew embraced "progress" with as much enthusiasm as any man of his day. If anything, his enthusiasm far exceeded that of other southern writers. Those who rose to prominence after his death especially displayed an ambivalence Dew largely had avoided. He reveled in the advances in learning, economic production, transportation, communications, even in morals, and he recognized the self-generating power of science and technology. Simply put, life was becoming qualitatively better for an ever-increasing number of men and women, and the root of this welcome progress lay in the expansion of individual freedom. Man, released from servitude and superstition, promoted enterprise, innovation, cultural improvement — in a word, progress. Western civilization stood alone among the great civilizations of the world in having found a way to break the cycle of flowering, stagnation, and decay by liberating the individual to pursue his own destiny within a Christian culture that provided a bulwark against the moral degeneration that marked previous epochs. The *Digest* might better have been entitled, in the manner of the English translation of Benedetto Croce's *Storia di libertà*, as *History as the Story of Liberty.* And who knows? Had it been, it might have sold a few more copies and might even be in print today.

For Dew, God provided harmony in nature and gave man the freedom of will to follow its laws. The sinful aspect of man's nature remained a serious impediment, but by devising free institutions he could promote the appropriate ways and means. His progress depended upon his socially secured freedom to pursue his own happiness in tandem with that of others. The necessary social security depended upon property rights, which had to be guaranteed by a state that protects the individual's right to dispose of his own property with as few restrictions as possible. To meet this responsibility the state must be firmly governed by propertied individuals under a constitution that restrains them from using their power at the expense of other propertied individuals; that is, it must be republican, democratic, and egalitarian.

Dew recognized democracy and egalitarianism only in the limited sense that applied to propertied individuals. He had no patience with the sweeping Jeffersonian formulations of the Declaration of Independence. He recognized neither the equality of races nor of individuals beyond that appropriate to the political life of those who owned property or, at least, respected its claims. Moral, intellectual, and material progress depended upon the special talents of superior individuals whose contributions depended on their release from drudgery. The progress of Western civilization has been spurred by the expansion of a freedom made possible by a class stratification that released some men to cultivate their talents. The expansion of the realm of freedom has generated economic and technological progress that has permitted the further expansion of freedom by reducing the amount of labor time necessary for the production of leisure. Freedom has become available to increasing numbers of men, whose combined efforts have resulted in an ever-quickening of progress. The course of progress and of freedom has remained upward and onward.

But could it continue? The laws of political economy, which Dew carefully studied and taught, pointed toward an unfolding tragedy. Dew pondered the ramifications of the Ricardian theories of rent, diminishing returns to agriculture, and the falling rate of profit, and he accepted Malthus's grim law of population. He concluded, as George Tucker did, that sooner or later, probably sooner, the cost of free labor would fall below that of slave labor and thereby inspire a widespread emancipation of slaves, as it had inspired the emancipation of the European serfs at the end of the Middle Ages. In short, the logic of Dew's political economy pointed toward the end of slavery.

George Tucker, unlike Dew, felt no trepidations. He concluded that slavery had no future and counseled the North to end its agitation and let the laws of political economy do their work. Tucker, arguably the ablest political economist in the United States and a man of generally humane temperament, easily swallowed the implications of the scenario: Slavery would disappear because the cost of free labor would fall and the living standards of laborers would sink to a subsistence level under a system that offered little or no protection during the periodic plunges well beneath that level. The great mass of mankind would have to live not only with poverty and brutal exploitation but with the threat of starvation.

Dew gagged. He regarded the outcome as morally unacceptable, as did the proslavery divines, who bemoaned it regularly in sermons, publications, and lectures to the academy and college courses many of them taught.[7] No Christian should be asked to live with it. Perhaps worse, the outcome was politically an invitation to catastrophe. Dew did not believe that the laboring classes would submit. He took the measure of the French Revolution and the even greater radicalism that it opened the floodgates to. His extraordinary chapter on the French Revolution in the *Digest* reads like a prophesy of the working-class rising of June, 1848, in Paris, which he did not live to see. Dew filled the *Digest*, from its opening discussions of ancient history to its closing comparison of the English and French revolutions, with analyses of the social movements he saw as a constant counterpoint to his principal theme of progress through freedom.

Erudite, deeply thoughtful, and temperamentally optimistic, if cautiously so, Dew delineated the dilemma. The very political and intellectual freedom that lay at the heart of all freedom produced and could only be sustained by economic freedom. Dew, who supported laissez-faire and denounced state interference in the market, recognized economic freedom as the special dynamic of material progress. But he feared that the story would end badly wherever the laws of the market were permitted to apply to labor-power — wherever free labor prevailed.

At the risk of distorting Dew's subtle and elegantly crafted analysis, we may reduce it to a few propositions. Freedom generated progress, which permitted a vast expansion of freedom. The extension of freedom to the economy, upon which all material progress has rested, meant submission to laws of economic development that condemned the laboring classes to unprecedented exploitation, immiseration, and periodic starvation. At the same time the historical unfolding of those laws required the extension of republican liberties that could not wholly, if at all, be denied to the laborers who had been removed from the security of their servile status and declared free men. Faced with unbearable privations, they would rise, were already rising, in insurrection. Worse, the intellectual freedom essential to all progress, including economic progress, was inexorably extruding every possible kind of utopian and demagogic scheme, which the revolution in communications was carrying to the desperate masses.

Like every other slaveholding intellectual, Dew denied that the laboring classes could consolidate a revolution and maintain power. They could, however, provoke anarchy and deprive the propertied classes of their power to rule. In the event, the capitalists, in particular, would turn to military despots, who would offer a minimum cradle-to-grave security to the laboring masses while protecting the propertied classes. But in so doing, the despots would have to destroy much of the intellectual, political, and economic freedom of the propertied classes. They would therefore undermine progress.

Dew ended by holding up the social system of the South as a model for a future world order. Only slavery or personal servitude in some form could guarantee republican liberties for the propertied, security for the propertyless, and stability for the state and society. Hence Dew faced a two-pronged dilemma, the ramifications of which he did not live to explore fully: Steady progress remained his great ideal; progress depended upon a regime of self-expanding freedom; a regime of self-expanding freedom provoked social conflicts that undermined it; and only the worldwide restoration of slavery could restore social stability and civilized order. What then of the self-generating progress that constituted the glory of Western civilization? The free market, once extended to labor-power, must end in perpetual civil war or the installation of despotism, but progress depended upon the extension of that very free market. Dew believed that the West faced a stark choice: It could continue a headlong progress that threatened to end in social catastrophe; or, it could effect a worldwide restoration of a servitude that threatened the end of civilization's progressive momentum. With a heavy heart he chose slavery, order, and stability.

His optimistic nature may well have led him to hope that material progress would continue, if at a much slower pace — that slavery, which he saw as the surest social foundation of republican liberty, would leave enough room for freedom of thought to do its work. After all, did not the South have a society free enough to participate in the progress of civilization? The problem nonetheless remained: Virtually all the great achievements associated with the extraordinary progress of the modern world had sprung from

the free-labor economies, and it did so for reasons he elaborated
as well as anyone in his work on political economy.

The dilemma had a second prong. The slave system of the
South faced a relentless foe, determined to settle accounts with it.
If Dew read the course of Western Europe accurately, the bourgeois countries would soon have to reinstitute their own forms of
slavery and thereby end their criticism of the South. But what of
the North? Dew saw the North on the same road that Britain and
Europe were treading. But its great territorial expansion and
peculiarly favorable social conditions promised to forestall the
dreaded outcome for centuries. Dew recognized the increasing
hostility to slavery in the North and feared a confrontation. If
the North, with its dynamic economy and potentially greater
military might, forced the issue, the South faced poor prospects.
Besides, even if the South did secede successfully, two hostile
regimes would face each other across a gun-bristling border. How
could republican freedom on either side survive under such conditions?

Dew took unionist ground and counseled the South to resist
provocations and eschew rash moves. His argument had many
echoes among the unionists of the South. But again, the problem
remained. If the North had centuries before it had to face its own
social question and reassess its attitude toward southern slavery, it
might very well become — indeed was rapidly becoming — more
belligerent and determined to force a showdown. How could the
South prepare itself economically and militarily without destroying the very fabric of its social system? Military might depended
upon that vaunted economic progress which the free-labor system
excelled in generating. Dew had an elegant formula: progress
through a widening freedom based upon slavery. But as he well
knew, if war came, formulaic elegance would not likely prove a
match for the big battalions, and, as he himself showed in fleshing
out the formula, the big battalions were likely to be on the side of
the enemy.

In making the relation of progress to freedom and slavery

the centerpiece of his life's work, Dew was focusing on the problem that increasingly was engaging the attention of thoughtful southerners. With few exceptions the lay and clerical intellectuals, in tandem with their fellow slaveholders, accepted both moral and material progress as the primary tendency in human history and as the unfolding of God's providence. But with varying degrees of emphasis they also recognized human conflict as inherent in that tendency, identifying the innate needs and egocentric practices of individuals as simultaneously its source and its social manifestation. In their own way they interpreted social conflict in the manner of a distinguished French historian who identified the cause of seventeenth-century peasant revolts as original sin and man's inability to live according to the laws of God.[8]

At this level of abstraction the slaveholders' view of progress could be accommodated, albeit with some tension, within the mainstream of modern liberal thought and its bourgeois-conservative variant. Even the special attention to racial stratification and the presumed right of a superior race to enslave an inferior offered nothing new or startling. So long as the slaveholders restricted their defense of social stratification, including slavery, to scriptural justification, legal sanction, historical ubiquity, and economic imperatives, they did not break decisively with the mainstream of transatlantic thought, and especially did not break with its bourgeois-conservative right flank. True, by the nineteenth century liberal thought generally condemned slavery on moral as well as economic grounds, but much bourgeois-conservative thought either did not or so qualified the moral condemnation as to draw its political teeth.

The dizzying outcome of the Mexican War, with its enormous territorial annexations, the projection of American power into the Pacific, and the discovery of gold in California, deepened the sense of progress, indeed of rapid progress, as the controlling law of modern civilization. Military considerations emerged as critical. In a world of aggressive nation-states and rival social and political systems, each participant had to keep abreast of the spiraling revolution in technology and economic performance or risk its life. One event after another taught the same lesson. The fate of Russia in the Crimean War, declared Thomas L. Clingman, the powerful politician from North Carolina, teaches the need for railroads and economic development as a matter of military survival.[9] Even the most "reactionary" of southerners — even George Fitzhugh — had to agree. Material progress would continue, whatever the wishes of those who lamented its pernicious effects. For slaveholders, as for the rest of humanity, the message was clear: Keep pace or die.

From self-proclaimed reactionaries like George Fitzhugh to such self-proclaimed progressives of Young America as Edwin DeLeon, proslavery southerners of every ideological hue invoked the rhetoric of human progress, sometimes with excruciating pomposity. Georgia and the South, exclaimed Whig and proslavery militant John M. Berrien in 1838, must progress under the banner "Onward! Onward!" The no less militantly proslavery Joseph A. Lumpkin, Chief Justice of the Supreme Court of Georgia, concurred, insisting that "the standstill doctrine must be forsaken, and forward, forward, be henceforth the watchword." The course of industrial progress cannot be arrested, he argued, and the slave system of the South must accommodate itself or disappear. "My motto," preached the Reverend Abednego Stephens of Nashville, "is — Upward — Onward!"[10]

Only a bit less flamboyantly, the famed oceanographer Matthew F. Maury of Virginia wrote Senator W. A. Graham of North Carolina in 1850, "Improvement and decay are alternatives. Nothing in the physical world is permitted to be in a state of rest and preservation too. When progress ceases, ruin follows. The moral world is governed by the same iron rule. Upward and onward, or downward and backward are the conditions which it imposes upon all individuals, societies, and institutions." Maury agreed with those who, like Rep. John H. Savage of Tennessee, viewed slavery as an essential element in the progress not only of the South but of the United States and the world. "With the possession of slaves," Savage told the House of Representatives in 1850, "the progress of this country has been onward and upward, with a power so mighty and a flight so rapid as to leave no doubt upon my mind but that the approving smiles of Providence have rested upon us." Calls to bold action normally invoked such language. Thus Francis W. Pickens, the wartime governor of South Carolina, exhorted in 1860: "You are obliged to go forward. You must increase, and the moment you stand still, it will be the law of your destiny to decay and die."[11]

More soberly, Frederick Adolphus Porcher took up the cudgels for a substantial number of southern intellectuals when he argued the modernist side of the regional version of The Battle of the Books. Writing in *Southern Quarterly Review* in 1852, Porcher, a prominent low-country planter who taught Belles Lettres at the College of Charleston, denounced those who wallowed in the glories of antiquity and eschewed those of the modern age. He expressed disgust at Hiram Powers's much admired statue of Calhoun in a Roman toga: "We asked for our statesman, and have received a Roman Senator. We asked for the citizen of the nineteenth century, and have received a specimen of the antique. We asked for our Calhoun, the Carolina Planter, and have received an elaborately carved stone." True conservatives, he insisted, want to guide change, not stifle it. "The great men of this world are they who live in advance of their age, and impress their mighty spirit upon that which succeeds them."[12]

Those who have read the slaveholders' voluminous diaries, letters, and personal papers must surely be struck by their celebration of the southern people as modern, forward-looking men and women, but also by their alarm at a world that was changing too fast and not entirely for the better. The alarm even carried into the pages of *DeBow's Review*, the leading organ of the celebrants of progress, whose upward-and-onward rhetoric could not disguise the deep uneasiness that pervaded all ranks of society. In particular, a belief in God and the deep piety that characterized many of the slaveholders — that "older religiousness of the South," as Richard Weaver called it — made them simultaneously hopeful, skeptical, and fearful that the modern world would suffer the fate of Sodom at the hands of the God of Wrath.[13]

The musings of Everard Green Baker, a planter of Panola, Mississippi, had parallels across the South. An admirer of Dr. Johnson, as many southerners were, he approvingly quoted a letter to Mrs. Thrale from the Hebrides, dutifully citing the appropriate passage in Boswell's *Life*. "Life," Dr. Johnson had written, "to be worthy of a rational being, must be always in progression, we must purpose to do more or better than in times past." Some months later Baker formulated his own view on the sinful nature of man: "strong & aspiring seeking to rise above the terrestrial greatness of all former beings like itself, & striving with that subtle intellect to peer into things which the wisdom of the great Creator has seen fit to shut out from mortals . . . "[14]

Nothing in Baker's papers suggests that he saw a contradiction between the two thoughts he entered in his diary or that he fretted over the tension. His Christianity, as expounded by the southern divines and integrated into the worldview of his community, taught him that the tension would prove creative so long as southern society adhered to the laws of God. The enemy was not progress, which was God's gift to his beloved children, but the cult of progress, which, as Baker observed, strove to project man to the center of the universe and to make man, not God, the measure of all things. Baker would surely have understood the message intended by the Maryland Institute in 1857, when it opened a series of lectures with the theme, "Slowness as a Law of Progress."[15]

If Baker had read William Gilmore Simms's *Woodcraft*, he would have had no trouble in grasping the point of a conversation between Captain Porgy and Sergeant Millhouse, who was offering to become his overseer. Porgy complained, "I was always one of that large class of planters who reap thistles from their planting." Millhouse replied:

That's because you never trusted to luck, cappin. You was always a-thinking to do something better than other people, and you wouldn't let nater [nature] alone. You was always a-hurrying nater, tell you wore her out; jest like those foolish mothers who give their children physic — dose after dose — one dose fightin agin the other, and nara one gitting a chance to work. Now, I'm a-thinking that the true way is to put the ground in order, and at the right time plant the seed, and then jest lie by, and look on, and see what the warm sun and the rain's guine to do for it. But you, I reckon, warn't patient enough to wait. You was always for pulling up the corn to see if it had sprouted; and for planting over jest when it was beginning to grow. I've known a-many of that sort of people, preticklarly among you wise people, and gentlemen born. It ain't reasonable to think that a man kin find new wisdom about everything; and them sort of people who talk so fine and strange, and sensible in a new way, about the business that has been practised ever since the world begun, they're always overdoing the business and working against nater. They're quite too knowing to give themselves a chance.

That's philosophy, Millhouse.

No, cappin, 'taint philosophy, but it's might good sense.[16]

A typical if unusually amusing illustration of the tension in southern thought over the very idea of progress in its relation to freedom came from Oxford, Georgia, in 1855. The Reverend William S. Sasnett, wishing to instruct his Methodist brethren on the responsibility of the church to keep up with the times, published a book on "progress," which he opened by declaring, "The development of the popular element peculiar to modern times, favored by the remarkable facilities for enterprise and expansion, has given, in the present day, signal activity to the spirit of progress." Immediately, he added a sentence he doubtless did not intend as a contribution to southern wit: "Progress, so far as it involves simply the ideas of alteration, modification, amendment, even as applied to Methodism, is not necessarily an evil." Change,

Sasnett explained, "is not necessarily to be resisted," for when subordinated to "thought and virtue, it is the glory of the age." He attacked government interference with that private initiative which constituted the great spur to progress, but expressed horror at the secular and infidel ideology that was being spawned by the initiative he was supposedly celebrating.[17]

Even George Fitzhugh agreed that the last two thousand years had exhibited "an aggregate of improvement." He hailed the slave South as a "bulwark against innovation and revolution" — "the sheet anchor of our institutions, which the restless and dissatisfied North would soon overturn, if left to govern alone." Yet in the very same article he complained, "Tide-water old fogyism retains its dogged do-nothing spirit." The conservative Virginia tidewater, he observed, opposed "railroads, canals, daily mails, and other modern innovations."[18] Fitzhugh especially admired Governor Henry Wise for his progressive spirit and dedicated *Cannibals All!* to him.

As J. D. B. DeBow and others complained, Fitzhugh loved paradoxes, loved to shock, loved to put-on-the-dog. But he also took himself seriously and meant to instruct. The intrinsically paradoxical nature of progress constituted his subject. "All civilization," he wrote, "consists in the successful pursuits of the mechanic arts. The country is most civilized which most excels in them." None of which prevented Fitzhugh from warning that the extension of railroads and other such wonders would reduce Virginia to the status of Ireland or the West Indies unless subjected to a wise, conservative regulation that controlled them in the interests of the prevailing slave society.[19]

For Fitzhugh, as for Everard Green Baker, material progress carried the promise of a better life, and, besides, it was inevitable. At issue was its rate and especially its specific content, for the dizzying rate made possible by the self-revolutionizing social and economic system of the transatlantic world threatened to unravel the fabric of civilization. Hence Fitzhugh's infuriatingly paradoxical rhetoric: "Slavery has truly become aggressive, ingressive, and progressive. It is the most distinguishing phenomenon of the reactionary conservative movement of our day." And again: "Let us show to the world that we, slaveholders, are the only conservatives; ready to lead a salutary reaction in morals, religion, and government; that we propose not to govern society less, but to govern it more."[20]

Few in the South could accept Fitzhugh's demand for increased state power, although many more might have if they had had the patience to follow his dialectics and smile at his irony. But then, sophisticated intellectuals and the less reflective country folk may well have intuitively espied Fitzhugh's backing-and-filling. Most southerners seem to have taken for granted that progress depended precisely on the individual freedom they claimed for themselves and agreed that only slavery could discipline individual freedom and thereby render progress morally wholesome and socially safe. But at that very moment transatlantic society, by dispensing with slavery and extending freedom to the laboring classes, was achieving unprecedented progress without the moral and social safeguards. Could, in fact, a modern slave society compete with such a rival in the all-out struggle that increasing numbers saw as just beyond the horizon?

As slave society slowly evolved from its origins in the seventeenth century to its flowering in the nineteenth, its statesmen, politicians, educators, jurists, ministers, and men of letters — in short, its political class and intelligentsia — increasingly recognized the challenge and continued to hope that it could meet the expected test of strength. Articulating the world view of the slaveholding class and, if more problematically, of the yeomanry and the middle classes of the towns, this impressive intelligentsia struggled to reconcile the claims of freedom and the legitimacy of slavery, and to find in their organic social relations a blueprint for ordered progress. On the relation of slavery to individual freedom and to moral and material progress, as on other matters of capital importance, a consensus emerged, notwithstanding its being wracked by the tensions, ambiguities, and quarrels that mark every worldview and social consensus.

In this case the tensions, ambiguities, and quarrels had a special root and quality that derived from a need to reconcile slavery with both freedom and progress. Ultimately, that reconciliation proved impossible, and much of the intellectual, ideological, and political warfare that constantly threatened to disrupt the consensus and unravel the worldview stemmed directly from its impossibility. At the heart of the boldest and most widely embraced of the projected solutions lay explosive contradictions that at last exposed a political dilemma and provoked a headlong plunge into uncharted and forbidding waters.

The contradictions especially signaled the southern intellectuals' determination to claim the Western tradition while criticizing the direction it was taking in Europe and the North, and while advancing their own vision of a healthy modernity. Every talented southern thinker proposed his own solution. The nature of moral progress and of the moral dimension of material progress — distinct if related issues — loomed large at the outset. Virtually all insisted that freedom and moral progress had to be understood not simply as the product of recent political developments, but as rooted in Christianity. The advent of Christianity had propelled the moral progress of mankind, and the spirit and doctrines of Christianity could be read backward in time to demonstrate moral tendencies in pre-Christian civilizations, most notably the Greek. The erudite even saw God's providence in such non-Western and non-Christian civilizations as those of China and India. How else, after all, should Protestants interpret the advent and spread of Christianity, the Reformation, and the missionary work that was going forward in Asia and Africa?

In this perspective, recent material progress was spreading moral progress, or so they interpreted the growth of the Christian missions to heathen lands. The wonders of the industrial revolution were having an especially powerful effect in the innovations in transportation and communications, which were carrying the Word of God to the four corners of the earth. In the words of the Reverend David F. Bittle of St. Michael's Lutheran Church in Rockingham County, Virginia, during the 1830s, and later president of Roanoke College, "As the sciences advance, literature becomes universal, governments become more tolerant — and improvements in the arts are continually making — is it not reasonable to suppose the facilities for propagating the cause of the redeemer will be increased and [that] new measures will hence constantly arise?"[21] Southerners, like northerners, generally identified the United States as the modern age's divinely favored nation and saw its rapid rise toward world power as evidence of its Christian mission. That rise revealed God's anointing of a chosen and Christian people. The freedom of the individual, the preachers cried out in unison, was Christ's gift to mankind. The doctrine of the immortality of the soul in the light of the Atonement made man a responsible moral agent and released his energies to perfect his being.[22]

The concept of moral progress nonetheless remained troubling. "The progress of Christianity," Albert Taylor Bledsoe reiterated after the war, "is the progress of man."[23] But if sin and depravity plagued mankind, as Bledsoe believed, then men might not progress to the point at which most, much less all, would be saved. The predestinarian Calvinists hardly expected any such progress, and even the Arminians entertained only the fragile hope that most would heed the call of Jesus. Together, Calvinists and Arminians, surveying the direction of events in the tumultuous nineteenth century, viewed the course of Western civilization with concern.[24]

The Rev. Dr. James Henley Thornwell, the most intellectually powerful of the southern divines, spoke for those of all denominations when he addressed the churches of the world in the wake of secession. The history of society, he wrote, serves as "the moral school of humanity," for God is in history and assigns each man his place.[25] In 1858, his fellow Presbyterian, the Reverend George D. Armstrong, pastor at Norfolk, Virginia, had struck a more somber note, but, then, he did not, at that moment, have to undertake the delicate political responsibility that fell to Thornwell under gathering war clouds. Reflecting on the consequences of original sin and the "sickness" of man, Armstrong wrote in *The Theology of Christian Experience*, "History, is to a very large extent, but a record of human crime." History reveals human nature as wracked by sin and beyond reformation through any philosophy: "Even where we have a record of civil or political reform, it usually presents itself baptized in blood."[26] Yet Armstrong wrote his book, as he wrote *The Christian Doctrine of Slavery*, to uplift humanity, not to denigrate it. The salvation of souls signaled by the spread of Christianity alone measured moral progress. Thornwell would not have disagreed. Armstrong never denied the fact, indeed the inevitability, of material progress, but, like Thornwell, he noted that it always and everywhere depended upon the servile labor of the great mass of mankind.

William F. Hutson of South Carolina expressed the ambivalence toward moral progress as well as anyone. As revolution was setting Europe afire in 1848, he wrote: "The history of the last seventy years has been a series of startling changes, and at the same time, of precocious and hot house growth, in art, science and politics — Europe, for the most part, has been a battle field; revolution has followed revolution so fast, that steam presses can hardly chronicle the shifting lines of states." Art and science, he continued, have rendered space "a mere mathematical term," and civilization has almost reached the refinements of ancient Rome. But toward what end? "What is the advantage we possess over the past? To the rich, have been added comforts, and appliances unknown to our fathers; but are the mass better fed? — better clothed? — happier? — more contented? — even freer?" Hutson saw an unfolding social crisis in Europe, which the United States could not long avoid. As for the qualitative dimension of moral progress, he summed up the dominant southern attitude: "In religion and morals, we doubt all improvements, not known to certain fishermen who lived eighteen hundred years ago."[27]

Henry William Ravenel of South Carolina, a respected botanist and unionist, offered reflections upon the secessionist hysteria of 1861 that, ironically, a host of secessionists might easily have agreed with while drawing opposite political conclusions:

> What a commentary does this spectacle afford upon the boasted civilization of the nineteenth century! It is too sad proof that with all the progress made in the *Arts* and *Sciences* — with all the writings of learned men upon *Civil Liberty*, and *Political Rights* — upon *Moral and Intellectual Philosophy* — with all the great *improvements* in *manufactures* and *material prosperity*, mankind are no better now than at any previous time — the evil passions of our fallen state are just as prominent and as easily brought into exercise as in those earlier times that we, in our self-sufficiency have called the *dark ages*. Nations like individuals become arrogant with power, and Might becomes Right. Egypt, Babylon, Ninevah, Persia, Rome have all learned the lesson, but we cannot profit by their example. We are working out our destiny. Deo duce.[28]

For Ravenel, as for Hutson, any rash assumptions about moral progress would have to contend with the inescapable evidence of the society about them: If the quality of moral life was the standard, then progress was hard to find. The southern divines, who did their best to discourage the hubris that claimed qualitative moral progress, evinced a strong, if little noticed, millennialism, although a millennialism largely shorn of the tendency to engage the church in campaigns for social reform. Methodists joined their Calvinist brethren in a literal reading of *The Revelation of St. John the Divine* and foresaw a Second Coming accompanied by social cataclysm and a battle of Armageddon. The southern divines' interpretations of the future varied, but they largely shared a sense of God's imminent intervention to purify a sinful world.[29]

The revolutionary upheavals in Europe, which began with the great revolution of 1789 and surged in 1830 and especially 1848, seized their imaginations. Individual divines differed as to which of the seals of *Revelation* was being opened, but they agreed that the Terror of 1793 and the June Days of 1848 marked the early stages of the prophesied cataclysm. In the wake of the working-class rising in Paris in 1848 and the radical turn in the European revolutions, the sober and politically sensitive Thornwell went scurrying back to *Revelation*, convinced that he was seeing the unfolding of its great prophecy.[30] In 1850 the *Tennessee Baptist* proclaimed that the European revolutions had ushered in the prophesied final battle of the nations. The Methodist Samuel Davies Baldwin, in his popular books *Armageddon* and *Dominion* and in extensive lecture tours with his colleague F. E. Pitt, interpreted the revolutions of 1848 as the "great earthquake" (*Revelation*, 16:18) that would usher in the final struggle. He predicted that the imminent battle of Armageddon would take place in the Mississippi Valley, not the Middle East, and related the expected triumph of American armies over European to the Second Coming of Christ.[31]

Not much imagination was required to translate this thinking into an interpretation of the slaveholders' confrontation with abolitionism as a war of Christ against Antichrist. Especially after the Mexican War, Thornwell and the most learned, temperate, and unionist of the southern divines, as well as the country preachers, repeatedly proclaimed the confrontation with abolitionism as one between a Christian people and the Antichrist. Yet before the War southern millennialism evinced a pronounced cheerfulness that would be replaced after Appomatox by the desperate hope that God would yet deliver his chosen southern people in a worldwide catastrophe. So long as the power of the Christian slaveholders waxed and especially as the prospects of a great new Christian southern nation loomed, the divines could see God's goodness manifested in the material and moral progress of Western civilization.

In that cheerful spirit the Reverend Benjamin Morgan Palmer of Charleston, uncle of a more eminent namesake, cried out in 1816, in a sermon aptly entitled "The Signs of the Times": "It seems as if everything [is] conspiring together in the moral and religious world and a multitude of things in the political world to introduce a new and better state."[32] In subsequent years the principal spokesmen of all the denominations read the signs of the times as a process of moral regeneration and material advancement that would hasten the millennium.

The study of history reinforced the prophecies of Scripture. Southern colleges encouraged the reading of d'Aubigné's history of the Reformation, which enjoyed wide circulation among the slaveholders and often turned up in their private libraries and accounts of the books they were reading. They read it as evidence of the progress of both Christianity and of social and political order.[33] Even the great history of the fall of the Roman Empire by the religious skeptic Edward Gibbon became popular in the South, where it was read for moral instruction despite its denigration of Christianity. For did not the barbarian invasions and the rise of Islam reveal the opening of the Seven Seals?[34]

Here too, the slaveholders' ambivalence toward material progress and the political dilemma it implied became apparent. As Christians, they saw moral progress in history in the wake of the "good news" of Jesus, however much one generation of divines after another stressed the inherent sinfulness of men, warned against backsliding, and thundered about God's wrath against a world too much of which resisted the message. And never had the good news spread so rapidly as at that very moment, carried by missionaries on the wings of a breathtaking revolution in transportation and communications and backed up by unprecedented military might. Yet that very industrial revolution was encouraging, with a no less unprecedented ferocity, a cult of scientism and an accompanying infidelity. New doctrines dared to raise man to the place reserved for God and thereby threatened moral decay and assaulted church and state, divinely ordained family and social relations, and God Himself.

Caveats notwithstanding, the slaveholders did place great weight on the quantitative progress of morality and did see material progress as its handmaiden. They thus linked Protestant Christianity to economic liberalism and political republicanism, much as a host of bourgeois liberals did. But in the slaveholders' perspective, slavery or, more precisely, the several forms of personal servitude, provided the necessary foundation for a society that could sustain a Christian social order and guarantee individual freedom for those who deserved and were competent to wield it.[35] They acknowledged that the greater the extent to which the individual found himself free to pursue his own destiny, the greater his contribution to the economic progress on which the pace, although not the content, of moral progress depended. And in this spirit they joined their liberal adversaries at home and abroad in embracing the claims of freedom as developed in classical political economy as well as in the emerging arguments for freedom of thought.

The southerners' warm praise of the benefits of freedom and progress have led many able historians, reviewing these and other matters, to attribute to the slaveholders a basically bourgeois worldview to which they merely tacked on an opportunistic defense of slave property and racial stratification. These historians have found irresistible the invitation to conflate the slaveholders' searing ambivalence with the kind of moral objections to the social devastation attendant upon unregulated capitalist development that were being heard in London, Paris, New York, and Boston, as well as in Charlottesville and Williamsburg, Columbia and Charleston, Huntsville and Mobile. They err, for the slaveholders, unlike conservatives in the North and abroad, explicitly identified the free-labor system itself as the source of the moral evils and forged a critique that struck at its heart.[36] With varying degrees of boldness, one after another came to view the freedom of labor as a brutal fiction that undermined the propertied classes' sense of responsibility for the moral and material welfare of society.

Despite similarities, only some of the important features of the reigning sensibility and worldview of the Old South may be assimilated to the broad current of conservatism that acted as a counterpoint to the increasingly dominant liberalism of the transatlantic world. In the North, in Britain, and most strikingly on the Continent, conservatives reacted forcefully against the high social costs of the industrial revolution, against radical-democratic and egalitarian social and political creeds, against secularization and the no less dangerous emergence of liberal theologies, and against the insidious pressures toward repudiation of church and family, authority and hierarchy, order and tradition. But for most, even their harshest critiques of the consequences of progress and individual freedom remained grounded in a fundamental acceptance of the reigning capitalist socioeconomic system. Some European and northern conservatives did assail capitalism itself, but they did so as isolated intellectuals who had been stripped of the social base on which the slaveholders stood.

The great divergence of southern thought from northern and transatlantic bourgeois thought, including its bourgeois-conservative variant, appeared in the confrontation with the specific nature of freedom and its implications for the present and future, most significantly the condition of laborers. Even the advocates of the extreme proslavery argument — of slavery as the natural and proper condition of all labor, regardless of race — understood freedom to entail a good deal more than their own claims to freedom as a privileged and preferred status. They acknowledged individual freedom as the motor force of a providential and potentially good historical progress. They simultaneously insisted that slavery afforded the best foundation for a free society.

The slaveholders' reaction against the ravaging consequences of bourgeois social relations had its counterparts in the radical-democratic and socialist onslaught of the Left and the nostalgia, lament, and harsh political response of the traditionalist Right, both of which condemned the moral irresponsibility and political corruption of the bourgeoisie. Unlike the radical democrats and socialists but very much like both traditionalist and bourgeois conservatives, the slaveholders feared the intrusion of the lower classes into politics and loathed the egalitarian doctrines that made it possible. Even when the slaveholders themselves invoked egalitarian rhetoric, as they loved to do at every Fourth of July barbecue, they implicitly, and often explicitly, suggested that equality and democracy could not be sustained outside a class-stratified system or its functional racial equivalent.

Thus at a first but deceptive glance, every southern denunciation of political radicalism, infidelity, and moral decay had its northern equivalent. To settle for a single illustration, the staunchly conservative Old School Presbyterian divines of both North and South, most notably Charles Hodge of Princeton, New Jersey, and James Henley Thornwell of Columbia, South Carolina, agreed on many of the important political and social, as well as theological and ecclesiastical, issues of the day. Yet, as the fierce battles between Hodge and Thornwell over church polity suggest, the issues on which they finally fell out exposed a widening and unbridgeable chasm in theology, worldview, and ultimately in sectional politics.

The break of southern conservativism away from northern in theology and ecclesiology accompanied the break in political theory. Partly as a reflection of a growing theological and ecclesiastical rift, the social conservatism of the southern divines diverged sharply from that of the northern divines. The theological, ecclesiastical, and sociopolitical conservatives of the North were steadily retreating in the face of the rise of Unitarianism in New England and of assorted forms of liberalism in the principal denominations. Meanwhile, orthodoxy continued to hold sway in the South.

The southern churches slowly drifted apart from the northern over theology and ecclesiology and by no means only over
slavery, for the northern churches were moving, if haltingly and
in intense internal struggle, toward more liberal positions on
original sin, human depravity, and the role of the laity. For immediate purposes, that larger sectional cleavage, notwithstanding its
enormous importance, may be left aside. More directly relevant
and illuminating was the growing estrangement of the theologically orthodox and socially conservative southerners from those
northern conservatives who were trying to arrest the liberal trend
in their own churches. The fierce polemics that pit James Henley
Thornwell, "the Calhoun of the Church," as he was called,
against Charles Hodge, doyen of the Old School conservative
Presbyterians of the North, may be taken as paradigmatic of the
sectionally based antagonisms that were developing within the
orthodox and conservative wings of most denominations.[37]

The issues concerned theology and ecclesiology first and
foremost and cannot be reduced to a projected ideological reflex
of sociopolitical differences. Nor was the slavery question, in its
direct political manifestation, the problem, for the northern conservatives condemned the abolitionists, opposed intervention in
southern affairs, defended southern state rights, and, in general,
resolutely insisted that the church must render unto Caesar that
which is Caesar's. Theologically, they conceded the main southern argument that the Bible sanctioned slavery, which therefore
could not be condemned as sinful, as *malum in se*. Slavery, in their
view, was strictly a civil, a political, question on which the church
could take no position.

In broader perspective, the slavery question did lie at the
root of the growing sectional antagonism within the conservative
clerical fold. Hodge provides a quintessential example. He denied
the sinfulness of slavery and defended southern rights so
staunchly that E. N. Elliott published his views in *Cotton Is King
and Pro-Slavery Arguments*, alongside those of Bledsoe, Harper,
Hammond, and other southern luminaries.[38] The conservative

divines, North and South, agreed that infidelity and social and political radicalism were on the ascendant — that the barbarians were at the gates. They agreed that abolitionism was a Trojan horse for all other detestable isms. They agreed that the fate of slavery should be left to the discretion of the white people of the South. They agreed on more. But they disagreed radically on the nature of a proper Christian social order and of the place of slavery within it.

The argument of the southern divines against the northern conservative divines took many forms, with variations and nuances, and it exhibited different degrees of political tartness. In the end it reduced to one point that brooked no compromise. And that point was made by the outstanding figures in all denominations: by Thornwell, Palmer, Adger, Armstrong, Dabney, Lyon, Ross, among the Presbyterians; by Smith, Brownlow, Pierce, Longstreet, Rivers, among the Methodists; by Stringfellow, Warren, Furman, among the Baptists; by others in virtually every denomination, including Unitarians like Theodore Clapp.

The point came to this: You northern conservatives share our revulsion against growing infidelity and secularism, against the rapid extension of the heresies of liberal theology, against the social and political abominations of egalitarianism and popular democracy, against the mounting assault on the family and upon the very principle of authority. You share our alarm at the growing popularity of the perverse doctrines of Enlightenment radicalism and the French Revolution — the doctrines of Voltaire, Rousseau, Paine. You share our fears for the fate of Western civilization. Yet you fail to identify the root of this massive theological, ecclesiastical, social, and political offensive against Christianity and the social order: the system of free labor that breeds egotism and extols personal license at the expense of all God-ordained authority. You fail to see that only the restoration of some form of personal servitude can arrest the moral decay of society. Indeed, you mindlessly celebrate free labor as a model and urge us to adopt it. In truth, the South stands virtually alone in the transatlantic world as a bastion of Christian social order because it rests upon a Christian social system. If, as you say, the world needs a social and moral order at once progressive yet conservative, dynamic yet regulated, republican yet immune to democratic demagogy, then our system, not yours, must be looked to as a model.

Thus the southern divines masterfully combined theological and socioeconomic arguments. Theologically, Calvinists and Arminians alike took a hard line on original sin and the depravity of man at a time when the mainstream churches of the North were retreating into rosier views of human nature and winning astonishing doctrinal concessions even from most northerners who claimed to be orthodox. The southerners developed an interdenominational social theory that stressed obedience to constituted authority, beginning with that of the male head of family and household, and they especially stressed the ubiquity and necessity of class stratification. At the same time they insisted, in a way completely different from that of northern conservatives, upon the moral duty of Christians to be their brothers' keepers.

Rejecting the kind of social reformism that was becoming popular in the North even among many conservatives, the southern divines insisted upon the solemn duty of the privileged classes to assume direct, personal responsibility for those whose labor supported society. Their rhetoric of family values had its northern equivalent, but with a decisive difference. In southern doctrine the family meant the extended household, defined to include "servants" — dependent laborers. The familiar expression, "my family, white and black," far from being a propagandistic ploy, expressed the essence of a worldview. For good reason Abraham loomed as the principal Old Testament figure among the slaveholders, much as Moses did among the slaves. Abraham was, in their oft-expressed view, simultaneously a great slaveholder and God's favored patriarch of a household that included his many slaves.[39]

From theology the southern divines frequently passed to political economy, which they readily invoked in their books and sermons and in their lectures to the college classes in Moral Philosophy. And with a handful of exceptions, the divines taught the generally required courses in Moral Philosophy. They accepted the principles of classical political economy, much as their northern counterparts did, but they broke decisively in their attitude toward the free-labor system itself. They refused to accept the outcome of Ricardian theories of rent, profit, wages and capital accumulation and Malthusian theory of population, which separately and together predicted the steady immiseration of the laboring classes. They were as ready as the northerners to accept the "laws" of political economy as operative in the market, but, an occasional George Tucker notwithstanding, they did not agree that immiseration exceeded the control of man. Jesus had said that the poor we would always have with us; he did not say that we ought to tolerate starvation and brutality. The system itself, after all, could be changed.

The southern divines' understanding of Christianity forbade a fatalistic capitulation to such monstrous laws and instead pointed them toward an alternate social system that functioned with more humane laws of its own. Sounding like Dew but with a greater sense of urgency, Thornwell and Armstrong, among others, insisted that the very horror of the laws of political economy could only end in proletarian revolution, anarchy, and a collapse into despotism unless the bourgeois societies assumed responsibility for their laborers through some form of "Christian slavery."

Joseph LeConte, one of the South's most distinguished scientists, summed up the argument in a lecture to the senior class of South Carolina College. A devout Presbyterian, he spoke primarily in secular accents, but the publication of his lecture in the prestigious *Southern Presbyterian Review* should occasion no surprise. By the 1850s such articles by both divines and laymen were readily receiving sanction in the leading religious journals. LeConte argued that sociology must be made scientific through the study of the natural sciences and the use of the comparative method in the study of human institutions. And he concluded:

> No one, I think, who has thoroughly grasped the great laws of development, or practised the method of comparison, will find any difficulty in perceiving that free competition in labor is necessarily a transition state; that, as a permanent condition, it is necessarily a failure; and that the alternative must eventually be between slavery and some form of organized labor, circumstances, perhaps beyond our control, determining which of these will prevail in different countries.[40]

The arguments were often ingenious and the presentations masterly, but the dilemma constantly resurfaced. Notwithstanding all caveats, qualifications, and ambivalence, the slaveholders, lay and clerical, sophisticated and simple, did want to preserve freedom, conventionally if ambiguously defined, and they did want to see progress continue. They extolled freedom as the source of progress. Thus, the Reverend William A. Scott of New Orleans wrote in 1851, "The history of Liberty—the history of the origin, rise, progress, conflicts, triumph and destiny of liberty—the history of men who have acquired their freedom—the history of those great movements in the world by which Liberty has been established, diffused, and perpetuated, is yet to be written."[41] Yet they insisted upon slavery as the only safe, secure, indeed Christian foundation for freedom, while they could not deny that the material progress they celebrated flowed from the performance of the societies that were not merely expanding freedom but eradicating slavery. Since those societies, in the view of American slaveholders as well as of European socialists, were failing and doomed to extinction; since for the slaveholders socialism was neither desirable nor possible; since some form of personal slavery would soon be the order of the day in Europe—how could progress be sustained? And more ominously, how could the slave South, notwithstanding its claims to moral superiority, stand against an aggressive North that had all the material advantages made possible by an unbridled free economy?

NOTES

1. Edmund Morgan, *American Slavery, American Freedom: The Ordeal of Colonial Virginia* (New York: Norton, 1975); David Brion Davis, *Slavery and Human Progress* (New York: Oxford University Press, 1984). Historians, including Michael O'Brien and David Moltke-Hansen — and the contributors to their volume, *Intellectual Life in Antebellum Charleston* (Knoxville: University of Tennessee Press, 1986) — Drew Faust, Kenneth Greenberg, James Oakes, Larry Tise, and Bertram Wyatt-Brown, have made illuminating contributions to our understanding of the slaveholders' views on progress, freedom, and slavery itself and have probed the relation of the one to the other. My debt to them is large, and my own effort to contribute to the discussion claims only that, so far as I can tell, none of these or other colleagues has focused on the link between freedom and progress and its implications for the defense of slavery.

2. For the slaveholders' view of the French revolution, compared with the view of northern and British conservatives, see Elizabeth Fox-Genovese and Eugene D. Genovese, "Political Virtue and the Lesson of the French Revolution: The View from the Slaveholding South," in Ronald Matthews, ed., *Virtue, Commerce and Corruption* (Lehigh, Penn.: Lehigh University Press, 1992).

3. Michael O'Brien has been exploring this theme in his several works. See esp. his remarks in the introduction to O'Brien, ed., *All Clever Men, Who Make Their Way: Critical Discourse in the Old South* (Fayetteville: University of Arkansas Press, 1982), pp. 24–25.

4. Consider such titles as Allen Tate, *Reactionary Essays on Poetry and Ideas* (New York: Scribner's, 1936); and M. E. Bradford, *The Reactionary Imperative: Essays Literary & Political* (Peru, Ill.: Sherwood Sugden & Co., 1990).

5. For an elaboration of the following discussion and the appropriate references see Eugene D. Genovese, *Western Civilization through Slaveholding Eyes: The Social and Historical Thought of Thomas Roderick Dew* (New Orleans: The Graduate School of Tulane University, 1986). For an excellent analysis of Dew's economic thought see Allen Kaufman, *Capitalism, Slavery, and Republican Values: American Political Economists, 1819–1848* (Austin: University of Texas Press, 1982); and for a particularly challenging interpretation that differs from my own see Alison Goodyear Freehling, *Drift toward Dissolution: The Virginia Slavery Debate of 1831–1832* (Baton Rouge: Louisiana State University Press, 1982), pp. 196–263.

6. Nathaniel Beverley Tucker, *A Series of Lectures on the Science of Government, Intended to Prepare the Student for the Study of the Constitution of the United States* (Philadelphia: Carey & Hart, 1845); St. George Tucker, *Blackstone's Commentaries, With Notes of Reference to the Constitution and Laws of the Federal Government of the United States and of the Commonwealth of Virginia* (5 vols.; Philadelphia: William Young Birch and Abraham Small, 1803); Henry St. George Tucker, *Blackstone's Commentaries for the Use of Students* (Winchester, Va.: Samuel H. Davis, 1926); *Commentaries on the Laws of Virginia, Comprising the Substance of a Course of Lectures Delivered at the Winchester Law School* (Winchester, Va.: Office of the Republican, 1831); *A Few Lectures on Natural Law* (Charlottesville, Va.: James Alexander, 1844); *Lectures on Government* (Charlottesville, Va.: James Alexander, 1844); *Lectures on Constitutional Law, for the Use of the Law Class at the University of Virginia* (Rich-

mond, Va.: Shepherd & Colin, 1843); R. H. Rivers, *Elements of Moral Philosophy* (Nashville, Tenn.: Southern Methodist Publishing House, 1859); William A. Smith, *Lectures on the Philosophy and Practice of Slavery, as Exhibited in the Institution of Domestic Slavery in the United States: With the Duties of Masters to Slaves* (Nashville, Tenn.: Stevenson & Evans, 1856). James H. Thornwell, *Discourses on Truth: Delivered in the Chapel of the South Carolina College* (New York: Robert Carter & Brothers, 1855).

7. Eugene D. Genovese and Elizabeth Fox-Genovese, "The Social Thought of the Antebellum Southern Divines," in Winifred B. Moore, Jr., and Joseph F. Tripp, eds., *Looking South: Chapters in the Story of an American Region* (New York: Greenwood Press, 1989), pp. 31–40; and "The Divine Sanction of Social Order: Religious Foundations of the Southern Slaveholders' World View," *Journal of the American Academy of Religion*, 55 (1987), 211–233. See also Mitchell Snay, "American Thought and Southern Distinctiveness: The Southern Clergy and the Sanctification of Slavery," *Civil War History*, 35 (1989), 311–328; and the works of Jack P. Maddex, Jr., cited *infra*.

8. Roland Mousnier, *Peasant Uprisings in Seventeenth-Century France, Russia, and China* (New York: Harper & Row, 1970), p. 306.

9. Thomas L. Clingman, *Selections from the Speeches and Writings of Hon. Thomas L. Clingman of North Carolina* (Raleigh, N.C.: John Nichols, 1877), p. 369.

10. John M. Berrien quoted in Stephen F. Miller, *The Bench and Bar of Georgia: Memoirs and Sketches* (2 vols.; Philadelphia: J. B. Lippincott, 1858), I, 54; Joseph H. Lumpkin, "Industrial Regeneration of the South," *DeBow's Review*, n.s., 5 (1852), 43; Rev. A. Stephens, *Address before the Academic Society of Nashville University on the Influence of Institutions for High Letters on the Mental and Moral Character of the Nation, and the Obligations of Government to Endow and Sustain Them* (Nashville, Tenn.: B. K. McKennie, 1938), p. 25.

11. Matthew F. Maury to W. A. Graham, Oct. 7, 1850, in J. G. deRoulhac Hamilton and Max R. Williams, Jr., eds., *The Papers of William Alexander Graham* (7 vols.; Raleigh, N.C.: State Department of Archives and History, 1957–1984), III, 409; Savage quoted in Arthur Alphonse Ekirch, *The Idea of Progress in America, 1815–1860* (New York: Columbia University Press, 1944), p. 236; Pickens quoted in William W. Freehling, *The Road to Disunion: Secessionists at Bay, 1776–1854* (New York: Oxford University Press, 1990), p. 461.

12. Frederick Adolphus Porcher, "Modern Art," in Michael O'Brien, ed., *All Clever Men, Who Make Their Way: Critical Discourse in the Old South* (Fayetteville: University of Arkansas Press, 1982), pp. 312–336.

13. Richard M. Weaver, "The Older Religiousness of the South," in George M. Curtus III and James J. Thompson, Jr., eds., *The Southern Essays of Richard M. Weaver* (Indianapolis: Liberty Press, 1987), pp. 14–27. See also Eugene D. Genovese and Elizabeth Fox-Genovese, "The Religious Foundations of Southern Slave Society," in Numan V. Bartley, ed., *The Evolution of Southern Culture* (Athens: University of Georgia Press, 1988), pp. 14–27.

14. Everard Green Baker Diary, July 22, 1858, and March 13, 1859, in the Southern Historical Collection of the University of North Carolina.

15. Patricia C. Click, *The Spirit of the Times: Amusements in Nineteenth-*

Century Baltimore, Norfolk, and Richmond (Charlottesville: University Press of Virginia, 1989), p. 30.

16. W. Gilmore Simms, *Woodcraft; or, Hawks about the Dovecote. A Story of the South at the Close of the Revolution* (New and rev. ed.; New York: Lovell, Coryell & Co., n.d.), p. 189.

17. William J. Sasnett, *Progress: Considered with Particular Reference to the Methodist Episcopal Church, South*, ed. T. O. Summers (Nashville, Tenn.: Southern Methodist Publishing House, 1855), pp. 7, 8, 61–64, 120, 135.

18. George Fitzhugh, "The Valleys of Virginia – the Rappahannock," *De-Bow's Review*, 26 (March 1859), 275.

19. Fitzhugh, "Make Home Attractive," *DeBow's Review*, 28 (June 1860), 625.

20. Fitzhugh, "Slavery Aggressions," *DeBow's Review*, 28 (Feb. 1860), 133, 138.

21. Quoted in Robert M. Calhoon, *Evangelicals and Conservatives in the Early South, 1740–1861* (Columbia: University of South Carolina Press, 1988), p. 159.

22. Stephen Elliott, the eminent bishop of the Protestant Episcopal Church of Georgia, expressed these ideas and tensions as well as anyone. See *Sermons by the Right Reverend Stephen Elliott, D. D., Late Bishop of Georgia, with a Memoir by Thomas M. Hanckel, Esq.* (New York: Pott & Amery, 1867), pp. xii, 1–10, 44, 47, 76–80, 117–127.

23. Quoted in John Joyce Bennett, "Albert Taylor Bledsoe: Social and Religious Controversialist of the Old South" (Ph.D. diss., Duke University, 1972), p. 49.

24. The extent and depth of Calvinist predestinarianism in the Old South has been grossly exaggerated by historians, but we may leave that matter aside. For immediate purposes it should suffice to note that even the orthodox Calvinists of the Presbyterian Old School interpreted the doctrines of atonement, sanctification, and justification in a manner consistent with the specifically political reading under discussion.

25. John B. Adger and John L. Girardeau, eds., *The Collected Writings of James Henley Thornwell* (4 vols.; Richmond, Va.: Presbyterian Committee of Publication, 1871–1873), IV, 461.

26. George D. Armstrong, *The Theology of Christian Experience, Designed as an Exposition of the "Common Faith" of the Church of God* (New York: C. Scribner, 1858), p. 161–162; see also *The Christian Doctrine of Slavery* (New York: Negro Universities Press, 1967 [1857]).

27. William F. Hutson, "The History of the Girondists, or Personal Memoirs of the Patriots of the French Revolution," *Southern Presbyterian Review*, 2 (1848), 398; "Fictitious Literature," *Southern Presbyterian Review*, 1 (1847), 78.

28. Arney Robinson Chiles, ed., *The Private Journal of Henry William Ravenel, 1859–1887* (Columbia: University of South Carolina Press, 1947), p. 67.

29. On southern millennialism see esp. Jack P. Maddex, Jr., "Proslavery Millennialism: Social Eschatology in Antebellum Southern Calvinism," *American Quarterly*, 31 (1979), 46–68; and "'The Southern Apostasy' Revisited: The Significance of Proslavery Christianity," *Marxist Perspectives*, no. 7 (1979), 132–141; and

Pamela Elwyn Thomas Colbenson, "Millennial Thought among Southern Evangelicals, 1830–1860" (Ph.D. diss., Georgia State University, 1980), esp. pp. 49, 70–71.

30. Thornwell to Matthew J. Williams, July 17, 1848, in B[enjamin] M. Palmer, *The Life and Letters of James Henley Thornwell* (Richmond, Va.: Whittet & Shepperson, 1875), pp. 309–311.

31. Samuel Davies Baldwin, *Armeggedon; or, The United States in Prophecy* (Nashville, Tenn.: E. Stevenson and F. A. Owen, 1845); *Dominion; Or, the Unity and Trinity of the Human Race; with the Divine Constitution of the World, and the Divine Rights of Shem, Ham, and Japheth* (Nashville, Tenn.: E. Stevenson and F. A. Owen, 1858); Colbenson, "Millennial Thought," esp. pp. 1, 12–14, 28, 49, 70–75, and p. 137 for the quotation from the *Tennessee Baptist.*

32. Quoted in Colbenson, "Millennial Thought," p. 1.

33. D'Aubigné was taught in southern seminaries and was introduced to students in the colleges. References turn up in the private papers of slaveholders across the South, particularly among the more religious. See, e.g., R. H. Kim, "The Seminary during the War between the States," in William A. R. Goodwin, ed., *History of the Theological Seminary in Virginia and Its Historical Background* (2 vols.; Rochester, N.Y.: DuBois Press, 1923–1924), II, 187; T. M. Garnett Diary, 1849; Diary of Lucy Wood Butler, Jan. 1 to May 4, 1863, in the L. W. Butler Papers; Samuel A. Agnew Diary, May 6, 1854, Jan. 4, 1863, Feb. 15, 1863, March 1, 1863; Franc M. Carmack Diary, Oct. 16, 23, 1852; W. P. McCorkle Diary, March 4, 1847 – all in the Southern Historical Collection at the University of North Carolina.

34. For a striking illustration see Bishop Elliott's sermon from *Romans* 1:16, which opens with a reference to Gibbon's "gorgeous" history: Elliott, *Sermons*, p. 44.

35. For elaborations see Eugene D. Genovese, *"Slavery Ordained of God": The Southern Slaveholders' View of Biblical History and Modern Politics* (Gettysburg, Pa.: Gettysburg College, 1985); Genovese and Fox-Genovese, "Social Thought of the Antebellum Southern Divines."

36. Elaboration and extensive documentation will appear in Fox-Genovese and Genovese, *The Mind of the Master Class*; for a small slice see Genovese, "South Carolina's Contribution to the Doctrine of Slavery in the Abstract," David R. Chesnutt and Clyde N. Wilson, eds., *The Meaning of South Carolina History: Essays in Honor of George C. Rogers, Jr.* (Columbia: University of South Carolina Press, 1990).

37. See Adger and Girardeau, eds., *Writings of Thornwell*, IV, which includes essays by Charles Hodge and Thomas Smyth, who broke with Thornwell on some important issues: Hodge, "Church Boards and Presbyterianism," IV, 242–295; and "Presbyterianism," IV, 616–632; Smyth, "Argument for Church Boards," IV, 581–615.

38. E. N. Elliott, ed., *Cotton Is King and Pro-Slavery Arguments* (New York: Negro Universities Press, 1969 [1860]). Hodge's contribution, "The Bible Argument on Slavery," is on pp. 841–877.

39. For an elaboration see Genovese, "'Our Family, White and Black': Family and Household in the Southern Slaveholders' World View," in Carol Bleser, ed., *In Joy and in Sorrow: Women, Family, and Marriage in the Victorian South, 1830–1900* (New York: Oxford University Press, 1991), pp. 69–87; for the specific nature of the southern household and its ideological ramifications see Fox-Genovese, *Within the Plantation Household: Black and White Women of the Old South* (Chapel Hill: University of North Carolina Press, 1988), esp. ch. 1.

40. Joseph LeConte, "The Relation of Organic Science to Sociology," *Southern Presbyterian Review*, 13 (1860), 59. On LeConte see Lester D. Stephens, *Joseph LeConte, Gentle Prophet of Evolution* (Baton Rouge: Louisiana State University Press, 1982); Theodore Dwight Bozeman, "Inductive and Deductive Politics: Science and Society in Antebellum Presbyterian Thought," *Journal of American History*, 64 (1977), 704–722; and James Oscar Farmer, Jr., *The Metaphysical Confederacy: James Henley Thornwell and the Synthesis of Southern Values* (Macon, Ga.: Mercer University Press, 1986), pp. 77–121. Farmer is also illuminating on his primary subject, Thornwell, and on much else.

41. William A. Scott, "The Progress of Civil Liberty," in Robert Gibbes Barnwell, ed., *The New-Orleans Book* (New Orleans: n.p., 1851), p. 48.

2

The Struggle for a Way Out

As early as the 1820s, but at an accelerating rate during the 1850s, the slaveholders confronted a widening gap between many of their cherished ideas and the exigencies of governing and defending their slaveholding society. For their society had developed in a republic that included powerful and increasingly hostile free states. Among the secular theorists, John C. Calhoun, like Dew, celebrated material progress and worried less than many of his contemporaries about its negative side. But then, contrary to the widespread misrepresentation that would have him a dour pessimist haunted by Calvinist predestinarianism, Calhoun flirted with Unitarianism and had a cautiously optimistic view of man and the future. He gloried in the great discoveries of science and the advance of technology: the compass and the revolution in navigation; the printing press and the spread of literacy; steampower, the magnetic telegraph, and the irreversible conquests of the industrial revolution. He especially singled out the diffusion of knowledge as an impetus to civilization "unexampled in the history of the world."[1]

Calhoun did not doubt that this vast material progress was engendering a better world. God surely had not given it to us for evil. Evils he saw but primarily as the short-run convulsions of the "transition," for governments had not yet learned to master the pace and content of progress.[2] Man had a bright future, but he had to learn patience and, above all, avoid the temptation to plunge into the wild social experiments that would transform the enormous good of material progress into a nightmare.

In defending slavery as a positive good, Calhoun preferred the politically wise course of restricting himself, so far as he could, to the specifics of black slavery. But, despite irate disclaimers, he could not avoid the higher ground of "slavery in the abstract." His writings and speeches make clear his belief that only slavery, in one or another form, could sustain republican government and the freedom upon which material as well as moral progress depended. Freedom, nonetheless, provided the direct impetus to progress:

> To perfect society, it is necessary to develop the faculties, intellectual and moral, with which man is endowed. But the mainspring to their development and, through this, to progress, improvement and civilization, with all their blessings, is the desire of individuals to better their condition. For this purpose liberty and security are indispensable.[3]

Calhoun's analysis and cautious optimism paralleled those of Dew in all essential respects. He, too, had forebodings, but he too expected the "transition" to end well, even if he never did identify the state toward which society was in transition. Progress for him was not merely inevitable but a joy. Freedom propelled progress. Republican institutions, better than all others, provided the security that freedom required. Slavery or personal servitude in some form offered the necessary basis for republican institutions and freedom itself. Yet, he regarded the "Hebrew Theocracy" as the greatest government man had ever experienced, and he held up the extended household, under the firm authority of its male head, as the model for social organization.[4] He saw no contradictions here. Freedom had no meaning apart from the social organization that alone could secure it, and the Abramic household, embracing servants as well as natural family, provided the best of possible social organizations.

Calhoun does not seem to have worried as much as Dew about the implications of the laws of political economy, which he interpreted much as Dew and other southern theorists did. That is, he, too, doubted that the free-labor system with its frightful exploitation of the laboring classes could survive. He, too, saw those societies in transition to some form of personal servitude appropriate to their discrete histories and circumstances. But he did not directly confront Dew's dilemma: If the free-labor societies were destined for convulsions, revolution, and anarchy, would not political despotism be on the agenda? And if so, did not the most advanced countries of the world face massive restrictions on freedom? What then would sustain the progress that depended, in the first instance, on the steady expansion of the realm of freedom?

In *A Disquisition on Government* Calhoun suggested that any answer must begin with a proper understanding of freedom. Focusing on the principal premise of modern political theory, he laid bare the heart of a long-building southern critique of liberal and bourgeois-conservative thought. "I assume," he wrote at the outset, "as an incontestable fact that man is so constituted as to be a social being. His inclinations and wants, physical and moral, irresistibly impel him to associate with his kind; and he has, accordingly, never been found, in any age or country, in any state other than the social."[5] In no other condition, he added, could men progress and develop their moral and intellectual faculties or raise themselves above the level of brutes.

Yet Calhoun insisted that man's individual feelings remain, despite such important exceptions as a mother's love for her child, stronger than his social feelings. In consequence, men place their own safety and happiness above those of the group and will readily war against each other when, as must occur, interests diverge. Two propositions stand out here: Man is driven by personal rather than social considerations; and man can only realize himself and his own freedom within society. Although sufficiently general to permit us to link these propositions to the doctrines of

Blackstone, Burke, and others, Calhoun's own doctrines, as steadily developed throughout his life, came close to a radical break even with Burke in their demonstration that freedom has no content apart from participation in society and acceptance of its restraints. The nature of that radical break and the essential difference in the content of the several doctrines are not obvious and require careful attention. Albert Taylor Bledsoe performed an invaluable service in developing the implications of the doctrine that had in fact become the basis of the emerging southern conservative worldview.

At the core of southern conservative theory lay a bold repudiation of the doctrine of natural rights or, as with Bledsoe and a few others, a redefinition of natural rights that looked like a repudiation to almost everyone else. Bledsoe, a theologian of parts as well as a political theorist, picked up the essential argument from Calhoun and pushed it to the limit. He attacked Hobbes, Locke, Blackstone, Burke, and others for their accommodation to bourgeois principles, and he forcefully reopened the question of the relation of the individual to society. A man who throve on controversy, Bledsoe drew heavy fire for some of his views, especially for his attempt to defend free will through a middle course between Calvinism and Arminianism. His political argument on the nature of freedom nonetheless resonated throughout southern writing on society and politics and explicitly and implicitly undergirded the defense of slavery. His argument also undergirded the critique of the bourgeois individualism that was infecting much of the nineteenth century.

Bledsoe led a full life. Among other things, he became a friend of Abraham Lincoln, with whom he crossed swords before the Illinois bar even as they worked together in the Whig party; he taught mathematics at Kenyon College and Miami University in Ohio and at the universities of Mississippi and Virginia; and he entered and left the ministry of the Protestant Episcopal Church, only to enter the Methodist ministry after the War. A good friend of Jefferson Davis, he had a stormy career as a secondary figure in the Confederate government and afterward wrote *Was Davis a Traitor?*, which ranks high among the expositions of southern constitutional theory. A Southron to his marrow, Bledsoe spent years at the universities of Mississippi and Virginia as a professor of mathematics, while he published on a wide variety of subjects.[6]

During the 1850s Bledsoe wrote two substantial books, which need to be read together for a full appreciation of his worldview. In *Theodicy* he subjected Calvinist and Arminian theology to searching criticism in an effort to defend free will and to clear God from the charge of being the author of evil. In *Liberty and Slavery* he replied at length to the scriptural as well as secular arguments of the abolitionists and vigorously defended southern slavery. Bledsoe was especially effective on the attack, but he succinctly laid out the constructive side of the southern conservative position on essential questions of political theory. Its theoretical core, shorn of the defense of slavery, stands by itself. We need not be surprised to find that Richard Weaver, the greatest of twentieth-century southern conservative social theorists, tried hard to resuscitate him.[7]

Bledsoe took up a theme shared by most if not all prominent British and American theorists. His critique of Blackstone may be taken as paradigmatic. Bledsoe went beyond the customary attack on liberal theory. He aimed some of his hardest blows at the bourgeois conservativism of his day. He made explicit what usually lay implicit in an emerging antibourgeois southern conservatism — that on certain essential questions even Burke had surrendered vital ground to the liberals. "It seems to have become a political maxim," Bledsoe wrote, "that civil liberty is no other than a certain portion of our natural liberty, which has been carved there from, and secured to us by the protection of the laws."[8] He thereupon pounced, implicitly when not explicitly, not only on Hobbes and Locke, Paley and Burlamaqui, but on Burke and Blackstone.

Locke, Blackstone, and most others, Bledsoe noted, saw natural liberty as a gift of God that distinguished man from lower animals. He quoted Blackstone as describing legal obedience and conformity to the laws as immeasurably more valuable than the wild and savage liberty sacrificed to obtain it. According to Blackstone and to virtually all modern theorists, the law restrains a man from doing "mischief" to his fellow man. The law therefore diminishes the natural liberty of mankind in order to substitute a more rational liberty appropriate to civilized life.

Bledsoe was incensed. How, he asked, could God give man a natural gift of savagery and of a wild disposition to do mischief to his fellows? Nothing in the Bible or in accord with common sense could support such an idea. "As no man possesses a natural right to do mischief," he retorted, "so the law which forbids it does not diminish the natural liberty of mankind. . . . The evil passions of men, from which proceed so many frightful tyrannies and wrongs, are not to be identified with their rights or liberties." Bledsoe countered Blackstone *e tutti quanti* by describing the law as a recognition of, not a limitation upon, man's rights by prohibiting the weak from oppressing the strong. Hence: "Civil society arises, not from a surrender of individual rights, but from the right originally possessed by all; nay, from a solemn duty originally imposed upon all by God himself—a duty which must be performed, whether the individual gives his consent or not."[9] Society, in short, does not restrain liberty. It creates it, and it does so primarily by restraining license.

Bledsoe parted company with Calhoun and almost all southern theorists in accepting the concept of natural rights. During the antebellum period his attempt to reconcile proslavery with natural rights looked increasingly idiosyncratic among proslavery theorists, being shared by James K. Paulding in the North and only a few others. Natural law was not here at issue. Thomas Cooper had little company in the South in rejecting natural law, and his position proved especially suspect since his claims to belief in God were reasonably scouted. Led by Calhoun, the southern theorists overwhelmingly accepted natural law but vehemently rejected the attempts to deduce natural rights from it.

Edmund Ruffin, who rarely acknowledged any proslavery tract as as good as his own, regarded *Liberty and Slavery* as grossly overrated, but he rendered one judgment that Fitzhugh and Bledsoe's other admirers should have appreciated. In a conversation with ex-governor George Gilmer of Georgia, Ruffin attacked Bledsoe for defending "the indefensible passage in the Declaration of Independence, that asserts that 'all men are born free and equal', instead of admitting it to be both false and foolish." Fitzhugh nonetheless praised Bledsoe for "hitting the nail on the head" with his critique of individualism, although he no doubt did not enjoy the remarks of James Stirling, an antislavery British traveler, who thought *Liberty and Slavery* better argued and less pretentious than *Sociology for the South*.[10] Bledsoe's acceptance of natural rights came from a man who was full of surprises. A rarity among southern theologians — and he deserves to rank among the ablest of southern theologians despite his checkered relation to the ministry — he abhorred the doctrine of original sin, notwithstanding his biting attacks on modern thought for denying or minimizing the sinful nature of man.

Bledsoe's views echoed across the South, although his direct influence is hard to gauge since many of those who shared his central idea of the relation of freedom to society may have come to it by a different route. In any case, such influential proslavery theorists as John Fletcher of Louisiana, whose work received widespread attention and praise, advanced similar if less precisely formulated views, as did T. R. R. Cobb of Georgia, James P. Holcombe of Virginia, and W. S. Grayson of Mississippi. The intellectual power of *Liberty and Slavery* received much favorable notice, and its place in the proslavery canon may be measured by E. N. Elliott's decision to republish it in *Cotton Is King and Pro-Slavery Arguments*. However much fire Bledsoe drew for playing odd-man-out with natural rights theory, he drew little for his insistence upon the social nature of individual freedom itself.[11]

A descent from the airier abstractions quickly reveals the ground that Bledsoe shared with his fellow southern theorists.

William F. Hutson, for example, scoffed at natural rights doctrine but ended in the same place Bledsoe did on the important issues. "We have searched in vain," he wrote, "for any authority for man's natural rights. If he had any, they existed before the fall." Any rights granted to Adam and Eve could not possibly have been "inalienable" since God revoked them. Society, he concluded, establishes rights and wrongs, subject to the laws of God.[12]

John Adger's argument, like that of other writers, had its special cast, but its ramifications hardly veered far from those of Bledsoe or Hutson. A Presbyterian minister, especially well known and respected in South Carolina, Adger wrote:

> The Creator originally destined man for society and civilization. These and not barbarism and personal savage independence, are his natural state. And consequently, all those rights and all those various subordinations of personal condition, which are necessary to the perfection of society and to the full development of humanity, are strictly and perfectly natural. That is as truly natural to which nature in its progress invariably conducts us, as that which is actually born with us.

It is a mistake, Adger added, to believe that because rights are natural they must be accorded to all human beings: "The rights of a father are natural, but they belong only to the fathers. Rights of property are natural, but they belong only to those who have property." Men have, he concluded, an equal and perfect right to the rights and privileges of the status to which they have been assigned.[13]

Had Bledsoe's proslavery critics read *Liberty and Slavery* with the care it continues to deserve, they would have had little reason to feel provoked. Bledsoe had a genius for redefining concepts virtually out of existence and then enlisting the residue in the service of his worldview. It would, for example, take little effort to demonstrate that, read in the context of his political theory as a whole, his indignant rejection of "slavery in the abstract" conceded the essentials of the doctrine he was purportedly rejecting. No wonder Fitzhugh let his gambit pass. Fitzhugh was not in the habit of quibbling over words and knew an ally when he saw one. Similarly, Bledsoe defended natural rights in such a way that those who blanched at the very concept found themselves in agreement with the conclusions he deduced from it.

Bledsoe ended with a powerful formulation of basic southern-conservative doctrine. The state, he insisted, must protect the "private liberty" of the individual. Even Fitzhugh, who wanted the world more governed, could swallow that much since Bledsoe added, "The rights of the individual are subordinate to those of the community. *An inalienable right is a right coupled with a duty; a duty with which no other obligation can interfere.*" Neither life nor liberty could qualify as inalienable rights since no conflict could arise between the rights of individuals and those of society, which alone gave form and content to individual rights.[14]

Bledsoe did not dwell on the relation of freedom to material progress, but his political theory, the essentials of which southern theorists shared, reinforced the interpretation espoused with special force by Dew. For Bledsoe, society could safely bestow political and civil liberty only on some, however much God could offer salvation to all. That those so privileged stood as the generators of material progress he never questioned. That those not privileged had to serve society by working for and submitting to the authority of the privileged he never questioned either. Others, more attentive to the debacle inherent in the unfolding laws of political economy could not so easily escape confrontation with Dew's dilemma. But if Bledsoe offered them only indirect guidance on that critical question, he did offer a political theory beautifully suited to their slaveholding worldview and to the work they had to do.

The most sophisticated southern intellectuals well understood that the twin doctrines of progress and freedom constituted the linchpin of bourgeois thought. Dew and Calhoun, especially, understood that it would likely prove impossible to arrest the self-revolutionizing course of scientific and technological development and to have both economic progress and the social stability that only slavery could guarantee. In embracing much of their social and political thought, not all southern intellectuals proved as unflinching or clearsighted. In this respect, the identification of progress with economic performance clouded the central issue. For at the most mundane level, progress could be associated with commodities that might be acquired without changing the fabric of life. Planters, after all, were delighted to buy the newly marketed sewing machines for use within their households without much considering that the industrial system that produced the sewing machines depended on free labor and spawned the values they opposed.[15]

Thus, even among the most thoughtful intellectuals, some assumed that they could have the benefits of progress without jeopardizing slavery. The main debate here concerned indigenous southern economic development, which many, notably J. D. B. DeBow, passionately supported. Could not the South do more to foster its own systems of transportation and communication and even manufacturing without putting slavery at risk? And beyond the practical problem lay the intellectual: Could not southern intellectuals borrow from the most important advances in bourgeois thought without threatening their own worldview and domestic arrangements?[16]

The leaders of southern economic thought — from the enormously talented George Tucker and Jacob N. Cardozo to such lesser political economists as Thomas Roderick Dew and on to such able popularizers as J. D. B. DeBow and Louisa Susanna McCord — happily embraced the classical political economy of Adam Smith, Jean-Baptiste Say, David Ricardo, and Thomas Malthus. They had much more on their minds than the justification of a free-trade policy for the staple-growing South. They were, with the exception of Tucker, trying to use the economic science of the age to justify claims to the moral and practical superiority of slavery as a social system.

The espousal of classical political economy in the South, manifested most clearly in the widespread commitment to international free trade, coexisted uneasily with the espousal of paternalism, manifested most clearly in the prevalent doctrine of the household as society's basic social and economic unit. The entire moral, religious, and social defense of slavery rested firmly on the notion that the laboring classes deserved cradle-to-grave security. "The first end of society," wrote Henry Hughes of Mississippi, "is the existence of all. Its second end is the progress of all. . . . Personal subsistence and personal security are the means of existence." Hughes's *Treatise on Sociology* won high praise from his pastor as well as from such secular writers as George Fitzhugh and William Gilmore Simms. His insistence upon minimal socioeconomic security as a basic human right drew few challenges even from men who found his general sociological system hard to swallow and who defended laissez-faire as proper economic policy.[17]

A commitment to cradle-to-grave security contradicted free-market assumptions, theory, and policy. Conversely, the possessive individualism preached by the great classical political economists from Adam Smith onward excluded slavery in theory, notwithstanding compromises on policy, and rested squarely upon the principle of every man's property in his own labor-power as well as his own body. Indeed, this doctrine necessarily applied to women as well as men, as such great political theorists as Hobbes and Locke clearly understood. The southern denunciation of Enlightenment liberalism as an invitation to sexual equality was therefore on the mark.[18]

The southern theorists nonetheless lived with the contradiction. For example, Louisa Susanna McCord, who ranked among the most confirmed of free-marketeers, staunchly defended both slavery and the subordination of women. Among her achievements, she introduced the work of Frédéric Bastiat into American discourse both through her translation of *Sophismes économiques* and in her articles and reviews for leading southern journals. Yet she squirmed under Bastiat's attack on slavery, which he classified with protectionism as great blights on American society.[19]

McCord's racism, extreme even by the standards of the Old South, helped her to avoid the implications of her simultaneous commitment to slavery and laissez-faire, for she simply assumed that whites should have to take their chances in the market, whereas blacks required special protection if they were to function as productive workers. Similarly, men like Robert Toombs could defend slavery as a morally and economically necessary system for blacks and yet oppose government aid to unemployed white workers as morally unsupportable and a violation of the laws of political economy. What made Hughes's views unpalatable to such men was his idiosyncratic insistence upon state regulation of the master-slave relation ("warrantor-warrantee" relation, as he preferred to call it). They saw no need to erect a Leviathan state, which qualified as one of their pet hates, to buttress a system of labor subordination.

Others, especially the more religious, could not fathom how a moral perspective that required succor and security for blacks could fail to embrace whites. Thus, from Dew and Calhoun to the theorists of "slavery in the abstract," they insisted upon a bifurcation of society that transcended the race question. Christian ethics and social safety required some form of personal servitude for all manual labor, and the laws of the market must be restricted to the sphere of commodity exchange. Freedom of competition, entrepreneurship, and capital must not be extended to labor. Human labor must be recognized as a social relation and never reduced to mere economic property — to the commodity "labor-power."

Hughes, like Dew and most other southern theorists, brought the question of "progress" to center stage. He, like others, saw freedom as the great spur to material progress, however much he departed from them in demanding an *étatisme* that would regulate and limit the economic as well as the social and political freedom of the individual. He began, therefore, where Dew had ended, in struggling to preserve the dynamic and progressive element in society while consigning the masses to strict subordination. He faced the problem of how to maintain progress, while, in the interests of social safety and social justice, curtailing the freedom upon which progress depends. He simply never conceded that progress required the expansion of freedom and insisted that the state-regulated freedom of a small ruling class would prove sufficient.

His peers blanched at the *étatisme* but increasingly embraced the notion that a dominant class could promote progress in a social system that denied freedom to its "mudsill." This proposed solution begged the question, for it did not so much refute the laws of political economy as try to bypass them. It fell silent on the original insight that the expansion of freedom to include labor provided the social foundation for the vast material progress of the modern world. A bemusing shift was occurring in southern intellectual life. By the 1850s the proslavery theorists, while continuing to invoke the laws of political economy to hammer the bourgeoisie, cooly ignored the implications of those laws for the future of slavery. In consequence, the intellectual defense of slavery quietly passed into the hands of sociologists, moral philosophers, political scientists, and theologians, who left the economists to restrict themselves to questions of policy rather than principle.[20] Like François Quesnay, the father of Physiocracy, the proslavery theorists ended, if metaphorically, by trying to square the circle.

Southerners in all walks of life pondered the prospects for slavery and debated whether God intended it to last forever. In so doing, they exposed the differences between their own notions of freedom and slavery and the notions prevalent in the North. And they inadvertently made clear that, for them, even emancipation would have little relation to the kind of freedom on which material progress depended. Laymen as well as divines pondered the very meaning of "forever." Did it mean until Judgment Day? until the onset of the millennium? until some time before the millennium when God gave a sign? The answers depended upon presuppositions. Premillennialists differed from postmillennialists, and the indecisive differed from both. To complicate matters, not everyone in each camp drew the same conclusions from the shared premises. Prominent divines like the Baptist Reverend Thornton Stringfellow of Virginia and the New School Presbyterian Reverend Frederick A. Ross of Alabama seem to have looked forward to emancipation of the blacks before the millennium, but, as with many others, they remained sufficiently vague to permit different readings of their work.

The problem appeared in especially acute form for those who invoked divine sanction for slavery as a social relation but focused primarily on the alleged inferiority of the black race. Among them, too, answers varied, with wide ramifications that would require careful analysis in an intellectual history of the Old South. Here, we may restrict ourselves to a problem that bears directly on the relation of freedom and slavery to progress in the world order the slaveholding theorists thought they saw emerging.

The future of slavery became a touchy subject, for by no means all leading southerners assumed or desired its perpetuity. A noticeable number of prominent clerical and secular writers looked toward some form of "emancipation," which they considered morally desirable and socially necessary. They sincerely believed that the abolition agitation was severely retarding the progress they hoped to see realized. Yet virtually to a man they defended slavery in principle as firmly as did those committed to the perpetuity of slavery. No deep, much less bitter, ideological and political split was occurring. The paradox disappears as soon as we recognize that the southerners' understanding of "emancipation" did not remotely carry with it the freedom that northerners associated with emancipation. In consequence, the specific progress in the condition of the blacks, which southerners associated with emancipation, promised little of that freedom which they associated with general material progress.

According to the Reverend Benjamin Morgan Palmer, who at the peak of his career held the Presbyterian pulpit in New Orleans, James Henley Thornwell was preparing a plan for gradual emancipation shortly before the secession of South Carolina.[21] Thornwell told Palmer that he had hoped to head off secession and war but discarded the idea as no longer practicable by the time of Lincoln's election. Palmer's memory may have been playing tricks with him, but if we assume that he was remembering aright, we would have no reason to think that the proslavery Thornwell had fallen into contradiction or bad faith. The apparent contradiction arises because Thornwell, at the very moment he reportedly was drawing up a plan for emancipation, was speaking out in defense not only of black slavery, but of slavery regardless of race. That is, Thornwell, denouncing the evils of the bourgeois societies of Europe, boldly predicted that they would soon have to reinstitute a social system so close to that of the South as to be indistinguishable from it. How, then, can we explain the coexistence of his proposal with his biblical views and his analysis of historical trends? We can in fact reconcile them and need not fret over the possibility that Palmer erred in his recollections of their conversation.

"There is no middle ground between slavery and freedom; no such thing as qualified freedom, or qualified slavery." Thus wrote T. R. R. Cobb of Georgia in his learned treatise on *The Law of Negro Slavery in the United States.*[22] Cobb was reviewing standard common-law doctrine, which one would think as clear as anything could be. Yet he displayed the apparent contradiction in Thornwell's position in slightly different form. Cobb, throughout the lengthy and learned essay on slavery in world history with which he introduced his treatise, insisted upon the ubiquity of slavery not only throughout world history but in the world of the nineteenth century. Reviewing the social systems of central and eastern Europe as well as of Asia and Africa, he noted the persistence of outright slavery and assimilated serfdom and other forms of dependent labor to a general concept of slavery. With the great majority of southern writers, he even denounced free labor as merely a disguised form of the general slavery that necessarily befell all laboring classes. Cobb was not arguing, as his remarks out of context might seem to imply, that men must be free or chattel. Rather, he was arguing that, juridically, men either were free to enjoy the full panoply of civil and political rights or they were condemned to one or another kind of servitude with human but not necessarily political and civil rights.

Cobb, Thornwell, and a vast array of southern social theorists explored the nature of freedom and of slavery, and some questioned whether the southern social system ought to be called slavery at all. Henry Hughes, William Gilmore Simms, and E. N. Elliott, among others, denied that it should. Others, like Thornwell and the leading divines of all denominations, would not quibble over the name but insisted that southern slaveholders claimed property only in the services, not the bodies, of their slaves. These and similar theoretical explorations led the slaveholding theorists, lay and clerical, to view freedom in an entirely different light than did northerners, including most of the ultra-conservative northerners who generally supported southern political positions.

Northerners, liberal, radical, and conservative, white and black, understood freedom as absolute property in oneself — as the logical opposite of personal servitude. Northern conservatives interpreted political rights in their own way but shared the basic premise of a bourgeois individualism that assumed the moral, juridical, and socioeconomic superiority of the free-labor system and the market. They thereby found themselves increasingly alienated from southern conservatives, whose notions of individual freedom were radically different and who restricted the market to the economic sphere. In particular, southerners, from social theorists to divines to politicians to ordinary slaveholders and yeomen, insisted fiercely that emancipation would cast blacks into a marketplace in which they could not compete and would condemn them to the fate of the Indians or worse. They meant what they said: The abolitionists are promoting genocide; we slaveholders, the Negro's best if not only friend, will not permit it.

Thornwell, then, might easily have proposed gradual emancipation without recanting his advocacy of slavery or his judgment that it represented the wave of the future in the bourgeois countries. For him and his fellow theorists "emancipation" could only mean the evolution of slavery into a system that continued to bind the laborers to individual "lords" while bestowing upon them important rights. In other words, it could only mean the sloughing off of the remains of specifically chattel slavery so that the laborers would be guaranteed a secure, legally sanctioned family life, would be taught to read, and would be protected at law against personal abuse. We may safely assume that such reforms were in Thornwell's mind because he and numerous other divines and laymen, including Cobb and such outstanding jurists as John Belton O'Neall of South Carolina, had long been advocating them.

During the War the advocates of reform steadily mounted attacks on the evils of southern slavery, which they had long acknowledged, and stepped up their demands for measures that would bring the southern system closer to biblical norms. Repeatedly the preachers warned that if the Confederacy did not institute such reforms, it might well face the wrath of God. We slaveholders, they cried, have been especially favored by God's grace — have been charged with the solemn duty to demonstrate that our divinely sanctioned slave system may be perfected to serve as a model of humane social relations. This war is testing us to prove that we are worthy of His trust. If we fail in our duty, He may well use the infidel Yankees to humble us, much as He used heathens to humble the ancient Israelites when He found them wanting.[23]

Calvin Wiley of North Carolina and James Lyon of Mississippi, among other outspoken reformers, defended slavery on scriptural grounds and pronounced it the moral condition of human society. They viewed their proposed reforms as perfecting, not overthrowing, it. Philip Lindsley and a host of others thought that slavery would survive into the millennium, but their understanding of "slavery" did not necessarily differ from the understanding that others had of a social state marked by "emancipation." Whatever the preferred term, the normal and necessary condition of labor was some form of personal servitude within the extended biblical model epitomized by Abraham. Call it "freedom," if you will, since it would no longer be the "chattel slavery" that antislavery critics thought they saw in the South and that even proslavery theorists recognized as at least a distorted remnant within the existing southern social system. One thing remains certain: The projected emancipation bore no resemblance to anything that northerners understood by freedom.

Thornwell thus did look forward to "emancipation" of a sort and to progress in human society. He did not contradict the notion of Dew and Calhoun that progress depended upon the expansion of individual freedom. But, like them, he never abandoned his commitment to personal servitude — to some form of "slavery," broadly understood — as the moral as well as the social foundation for a civilized society. Nor could he abandon it, for his reading of history and political economy left him no choice. And, more important, in his reading of the Bible, "the mouth of the Lord hath spoken it."

The freedom that Dew, Calhoun, Thornwell, and their contemporaries viewed as essential to progress included freedom of thought and speech, which they especially valued. But their society lay embedded in a larger and increasingly hostile transatlantic bourgeois world. They could not even try to shut out the values and dangerous propaganda of that larger world without drastically curtailing the freedom of speech they regarded as essential to freedom in general and therefore to progress. With mounting vehemence, the slaveholders demanded that the North suppress, even hang, abolitionists. All attacks on slavery threatened social order and must be declared beyond the pale. Even Dew called for antiabolitionist measures, forgetting that he had long ridiculed the old regimes of Europe for suppressing criticisms of basic social relations. What else, he demanded to know, was worthy of serious discussion? Freedom of speech, he stoutly maintained, must especially include the right to level fundamental criticisms of the social order. In failing to meet that acid test, the slaveholders and Dew himself rendered a harsh judgment on their favorite notion that only slavery could sustain republican values.[24]

Southerners did not much discuss the limits of free speech, at least not in a theoretical way, but they did impose a good deal of self-censorship on themselves, especially after 1831. Prominent proslavery divines sometimes decided not to publish sermons that made the common and generally acceptable call for more humane treatment of slaves, when they feared that even proslavery sermons might be misconstrued at moments of high political temper. Few if any voices rose to defend those who attacked slavery and then met violence. Political moderates and their newspapers — Jacob N. Cardozo of Charleston and his *Southern Patriot* may stand for many others — indignantly supported measures to suppress abolitionists and their publications in both North and South. Clement Eaton, in his *Freedom-of-Thought Struggle in the Old South*, has documented the depressing story of a war against freedom of speech, but that war was more narrowly circumscribed than he and other historians have allowed. Southerners who remained within the proslavery consensus enjoyed a degree of free speech that might easily have been envied anywhere in Europe, not to mention the rest of the world. Southerners remained convinced that the individual could not pursue his own destiny and realize his social "usefulness" in other than an atmosphere of freedom of thought.[25]

Southern intellectuals and the slaveholders as a class believed in republican freedom and drew the line only against those who, in their estimation, threatened its social foundation. They professed to believe in the spirit as well as the letter of the Bill of Rights, for which they claimed principal credit, and they certainly believed that freedom must be preserved if the progress to which they were committed was to be maintained. They did not much discuss the issue because they saw little to discuss. As men who stood for a well-ordered Christian progress in both material and moral affairs, they simply took for granted that free thought and free speech were indispensable for the promotion of men's happiness and well-being. But as men who felt themselves beleaguered in a hostile world, they reflected little on the implications of their suppression of criticism of slavery.

When they did touch upon the subject, they almost invariably did so in order to remind their readers of the social necessity of freedom, as well as its sanction in Christian doctrine. William Gilmore Simms made the classic argument, "It is the artist only who is the true historian . . . . We care not so much for the intrinsic truth of history, as for the great moral truths, which, drawn from such sources, induce excellence in the student."[26] Simms expressed the widely held Jeffersonian view that an author need not be correct in his conjectures, assertions, and themes, so long as others remained free to refute him. Simms and his peers, whatever their lapses in practice, claimed this basic liberal doctrine as their own.

Simms, like other proslavery theorists, acknowledged no contradiction between a commitment to maximum intellectual freedom and a commitment to slavery. To the contrary, he, like the rest, including his friend James Henry Hammond, believed that the one required the other. Thus Simms welcomed Hughes's *Treatise on Sociology*, which called for state supervision of the subordination of all labor regardless of race to the authority of individual "warrantors." The *Treatise*, Simms wrote, is the product of "a profound, searching, exhilarating, well-drilled and highly logical mind; a deep, close, and discriminating faculty of thought; and a perfectly honest, as it is a perfectly conclusive argument."[27]

Although Simms proudly proclaimed himself a democrat and long supported some of the more radical tendencies in the Democratic party and "Young America," he accepted the need for social stratification and for the rigid subordination of the laboring classes. In twenty years, he wrote William Alfred Jones in 1851, our republic will split, and the South will emerge as the stronger, safer, more stable of the two countries: "In the North, you are all rivals, in the same occupations, and overrun besides with the desperates of Europe who will be then numerous enough to perfect their doctrines of licentiousness, by covering you with the curse of Agrarianism. You have nothing conservative in your morals and institutions."[28]

In 1858, Simms urged Hammond to inspire fear in men: "The great body of mankind are exceedingly curlike, and the stroke of the whip, which rouses the noble nature to fury, only compels the masses to lick the hand that scourges." Two years later he wrote James Lawson, "The great majority of mankind is born to poverty & toil." He was referring to white as well as black men. Arguably, Simms swung rightward and got crankier as he grew older, but the views on man and society he expressed publicly and privately in the 1850s differed in no essential respect from those he had expressed in his polemic on "The Morals of Slavery" in the 1830s.[29]

These themes and ideological tendencies — this worldview — contained a broadside assault on Jacobinism, socialism, and all forms of radical democracy and a remarkably frank defense of a politics that could accommodate a stratified social order. The survival of the much invoked Burkean "manly and well-regulated liberty" rested, in this southern interpretation, upon slavery itself, or at least upon some roughly equivalent form of personal servitude for the laboring or "mudsill" classes. The slaveholders' worldview appeared in the work of the South's leading men and women of letters, including novelists like Simms himself and the formidable Augusta Jane Evans, but here we shall have to restrict ourselves to a few poets who, thanks largely to the Yankee bias that dominates the writing of history, have fallen into undeserved obscurity.

The slaveholders' worldview, with its formula of progress through freedom under slavery, enlisted the talents of the best southern poets, including Edgar Allan Poe and others whose best work stands up well against that of the northerners who have eclipsed them — at least if we except the great Emily Dickinson. Consider two gifted citizens of Georgia, Richard Henry Wilde, whose "My Life Is Like the Summer Rose" Lord Byron is reported to have declared the finest poem he had seen come out of America, and the mercurial Thomas Holley Chivers, who enjoyed a fine reputation in New England as well as the South.[30] Neither Wilde nor Chivers turned their poetry into a platform for southern causes, however much their poetry may have expressed specifically southern sensibilities. But Wilde, especially as a member of the United States Congress, and Chivers, especially as a contributor to Georgia newspapers from the vantage point of a longtime residence in New England, staunchly upheld southern rights and slavery in their prose. They did so, in part, with withering attacks on the social system of the North, not merely on its political policies. With a jaundiced eye on conditions in Britain, Wilde declared in 1825, "The Southern States are already the Ireland of the Union."[31]

Chivers did write "political" poetry, but it celebrated America, not specifically the South. He wrote to extol America as God's chosen land of freedom and the vanguard of world progress. In the words of his biographer, Charles Henry Watts, Chivers's poems "spoke in large terms of the nature of liberty, of the magnificence and destiny of his country, and of the strength of her heroes."[32] Chivers preferred to live amidst the vibrant urban social and intellectual life of the Northeast, in part because he appreciated its greater sexual freedom. His personal life did not accord well with the sensibility of small-town life in Georgia. Chivers never hid his admiration for the greater personal and artistic freedom of life in the North, nor did he spare the South biting criticism for its unwillingness or inability to sustain a sizable community of poets and other artists. He had no trouble in seeing that greater freedom as the basis for the North's envied rate of material progress. Yet he excoriated the social system of the North and unswervingly upheld that of the South. In particular, he wrote indignant accounts of northern labor conditions, including those faced by the "factory girls" of Lowell. There seems to have been no question in his mind that the very freedom he admired and sought for himself in the North carried with it the horrible oppression of the laboring classes, the denigration of women, and the creeping dissolution of civilized social life. He stood firmly with his state, even if he did not much enjoy life there.

Ideological differences among southern men of letters surfaced in the literary debates, most notably the debate between William J. Grayson and Henry Timrod in Charleston. Aesthetics not sociology, poetry not history, constituted the terrain of intellectual struggle, but contemporaries, prefiguring subsequent historians and literary critics, discerned political and ideological implications. The debate pitted a traditionalist defender of classicism against a romantic exponent of modernity, and appropriately, as David Moltke-Hansen has stressed, it pitted an older against a younger man in a marked shift of generational sensibility. Although low-country gentlemen and friends, their polemics sometimes got sharp, and Timrod, in an uncharacteristic outburst, referred to Grayson as of "the old fossil school." But the struggle over aesthetics did not betoken a deep political rift.[33]

Neither Timrod nor Grayson tried to turn their differences into a political brawl, notwithstanding Grayson's sense of a dangerous correlation between the aesthetics of the younger generation and the lamentable tendency toward the political extremism and social disintegration he saw on the rise. True, as might be expected, Timrod took the more radical political stance, although he was, if anything, more diffident than Grayson about making political pronouncements. In effect, two types of conservatism confronted one another, for Grayson, Timrod, and their respective allies considered themselves, and in fact were, strong supporters of the southern social order. Timrod, who adjusted to secession much more easily than Grayson, qualified as a unionist until the eleventh hour, agreeing with Grayson and many other unionists that slavery would be much safer in rather than out of the Union.

Both Grayson and Timrod took high ground in defense of slavery, regarding it as a social system immeasurably superior to the social system based on free labor that prevailed in Britain and the North and was steadily advancing on the European continent. Once the South crossed the Rubicon of secession, Timrod raised the standard of a revolutionary transformation and proclaimed the southern social system a model for a morally and aesthetically superior world order. A socially responsible Christian ruling class would provide the laboring classes of the world with a decent and secure life.

When George Fitzhugh proclaimed, "We want no new world!" Timrod and romantics like him could say Amen! for they too stood on traditionalist Christian ground and prophesied a worldwide restoration of much of an older social order. But they simultaneously sought to preserve much of the accomplishments of modernity, especially its celebration of the individual, albeit within a stratified society. To accomplish that feat, they envisioned not a restoration of ancient slavery or medieval serfdom, but the perfection of a modern servitude that transformed slavery into a more recognizably Christian and humane system and spread it throughout the world by the force of its example. In this sense they stood for a dramatically new world. And however deep their racism and readiness to consign blacks as a people to inferior status, racial stratification per se did not constitute the heart of their project.

In February 1861, as the first Confederate Congress met in Montgomery, Alabama, Timrod wrote "Ethnogenesis" to celebrate the birth of a new nation dedicated to the creation of a new world order. The last stanza contains the lines:

> But let our fears — if fears we have — be still,
> And turn us to the future! Could we climb
> Some mighty Alp, and view the coming time,

The rapturous sight would fill
    Our eyes with happy tears!
Not only for the glories which the years
Shall bring us; not from lands from sea to sea,
And wealth, and power, and peace, though these
    shall be;
But for the distant peoples we shall bless,
And the hushed murmurs of a world's distress:
For, to give labor to the poor,
    The whole sad planet o'er,
And save from want and crime the humblest door,
Is one among the many ends for which
    God makes us great and rich![34]

Timrod had company across the South in extending
Grayson's assault on capitalism and defense of slavery as a superior social system. In Mississippi, for example, J. S. Morris, a
prominent lawyer and a poet of questionable ability, accepted an
invitation to submit a poem for the commencement at Oakland
College in 1858. Echoing Grayson and foreshadowing Timrod,
he wrote:

Of Anglo-Southern men, by whom t'is God's design
To conquer, elevate and rule the heathen hosts,
Who groan in pagan chains on Afric's torrid coast . . .
Though England and the North, with heart of frozen
    snow,
Forget their home-born hireling, starving, brothers'
    woe,
And envious of our hopes, with insolence may rave
Of tortures which they dream are suffered by the
    slave . . . [35]

Grayson kept a closer eye on political realities and showed
greater awareness of the strength of the antislavery forces on both
sides of the ocean. He went to great lengths to deny that he

sought to export the southern slave system or to recommend it to others. He insisted that he sought only to justify black slavery in time and place and to ask others to solve their own problems in their own ways. But he could not maintain that position even in his polemical preface to "The Hireling and the Slave," and the poem itself belied those modest claims.[36] For in the poem he extolled slavery as morally and materially superior to the free-labor system, which he unmistakably condemned as vicious and politically unstable. Caution and restrained rhetoric notwithstanding, he established the ideological groundwork for Timrod's bold advance to an explicit proclamation of a southern slaveholding Confederacy that would lead the world.

Grayson took a dim view of the future and did not hold southern slavery up as a model. Indeed, he believed as readily in 1861 as he had earlier that secession and war would spell the death of slavery. He regarded the Union as the world's greatest experiment in free government and saw the approaching war as an unfolding tragedy. Despite all such gnashing of teeth, Grayson entered, if gloomily, on the very terrain Timrod occupied cheerfully. Consider Grayson's paean to southern slavery in *The Letters of Curtius:*

> Slave labor is the only organized labor ever known. It is the only condition of society in which labor and capital are associated on a large scale in which their interests are combined and not in conflict. Every plantation is an organized community, a phalanstery, as Fourier would call it—where all work, where each member gets subsistence and a home and the more industrious larger pay and profits to their own superior industry.[37]

Here, as in "The Hireling and the Slave" and his autobiography, Grayson did not merely contrast slavery favorably with free labor; he condemned free labor as a system at once inhumane, unstable, and destructive of civilized values. Since he constantly extolled slavery as a moral and humane social foundation for civilized values, he differed from Timrod principally in his lack of faith in the South's ability to sustain itself as a slaveholding republic. Like Dew and Hammond, among others, Grayson understood the power of a freedom that simultaneously generated and corrupted material progress. And with that understanding went a deep foreboding that progress, however deeply corrupted by immorality and political degradation, would pursue its relentless course against a South unable to stand.

NOTES

1. John C. Calhoun, *A Disquisition on Government and Selections from the Discourse* (Indianapolis: Bobbs-Merrill, 1953), p. 67, and, generally, pp. 66–69. Calhoun's ideas on these questions run throughout his life's work but were most clearly and succinctly stated in the *Disquisition.*
2. Calhoun, *Disquisition,* pp. 68–69.
3. Calhoun, *Disquisition,* p. 40.
4. For Calhoun's views on the "Hebrew Theocracy," as reported by Augustus Baldwin Longstreet, see John Donald Wade, *Augustus Baldwin Longstreet: A Study in the Development of Culture in the Old South* (New York: Macmillan, 1924), p. 60. In 1844, Calhoun wrote a fierce letter to his political supporters in Ohio to counter the damaging charge that he regarded slavery as the natural and proper condition for all labor. Calhoun used strong language: "utterly destitute of the shadow of truth"; "utterly false"; "a calumny, utterly destitute of foundation." Calhoun retorted that he was being maligned by Whigs and that he had an unblemished record of extolling freedom. He charged that the Whigs were attacking him for having exposed their economic program as leading toward the enslavement of the white working class. Hammond, among many other politically vulnerable southerners, made a similar disclaimer, which will be examined in chapter three, *infra.* A full discussion of these disclaimers, their form, significance, and bad faith will have to await an appropriate moment. But it should be enough to note that Calhoun repeatedly pointed to slave society, ancient as well as modern, as the best form of human community and the best foundation for republican government. I am indebted to Clyde Wilson for drawing my attention to this letter, which he has published in volume 19 of his splendid edition of Calhoun's works. See John C. Calhoun to Robert I. Alexander and Others, St. Clairsville, Ohio, Sept. 11, 1844, in Robert L. Merriwether, W. Edwin Hemphill, and Clyde N. Wilson, eds., *The Papers of John C. Calhoun* (20 vols. to date; Columbia: University of South Carolina Press, 1959–), XIX, 757–759.
5. Calhoun, *Disquisition,* p. 3.
6. On Bledsoe see the appraisals of Richard M. Weaver in Curtis and Thompson, eds., *The Southern Essays of Richard M. Weaver,* pp. 147–158; and

Weaver, *The Southern Tradition at Bay: A History of Postbellum Thought* (New York: Arlington House, 1968), pp. 115–122, 133–138, 143–145, 153–161, and *passim;* Bennett, "Albert Taylor Bledsoe," and Bennett, "Albert Taylor Bledsoe: Transitional Philosopher of the Old South," *Methodist History*, 11 (1972), 3–14. Also Samuel Marx Barton, "The South's Contribution to Mathematics and Astronomy," in Julian Alvin Carroll Chandler, et al., eds., *The South in the Building of the Nation* (13 vols.; Richmond, Va.: Southern Historical Publication Society, 1909–1913), VII, 205; Philip Alexander Bruce, *History of the University of Virginia: The Lengthened Shadow of One Man* (5 vols.; New York: Macmillan, 1920–1922), III, 38, 79–81, 142, 262, 344; IV, 27.

7. Bledsoe, *A Theodicy; or, Vindication of the Divine Glory, as Manifested in the Constitution and Government of the Moral World* (New York: Nelson & Phillips, 1853); and Bledsoe, *An Essay on Liberty and Slavery* (Philadelphia: J. B. Lippincott, 1857).

8. Bledsoe, *Liberty and Slavery*, p. 13, and, generally, pp. 12–34.

9. Bledsoe, *Liberty and Slavery*, pp. 18, 19, 28.

10. William Kauffman Scarborough, ed., *The Diary of Edmund Ruffin* (3 vols.; Baton Rouge: Louisiana State University Press, 1972–1989), I, 90, 140; Fitzhugh, "Oliver Goldsmith and Doctor Johnson," *DeBow's Review*, 28 (1860), 513; James Stirling, *Letters from the Slave States* (New York: Negro Universities Press, 1969 [1857]), pp. 111–112, 117.

11. John Fletcher, *Studies on Slavery, in Easy Lessons* (Natchez, Miss.: Jackson Warner, 1852); Thomas R. R. Cobb, *The Law of Negro Slavery in the United States, to Which is Prefixed, An Historical Sketch of Slavery* (New York: Negro Universities Press, 1968 [1858]), see esp. the Historical Sketch, pp. xxxv–ccviii; W. S. Grayson, "Natural Equality of Man," *DeBow's Review*, 26 (Jan. 1859), 29–38.

12. Hutson, "History of the Girondists," 401.

13. John Adger, "The Christian Doctrine of Human Rights and Slavery," *Southern Presbyterian Review*, 2 (1848–1849), 570, 571.

14. Bledsoe, *Liberty and Slavery*, p. 38.

15. As James Oakes has sardonically observed, although the slaveholders "attributed regal powers to the cotton crop," cotton was "pawn, not king," in its relation to transatlantic capitalism. See *Slavery and Freedom: An Interpretation of the Old South*.

16. On DeBow's economic thought and ideology see Thanet.Aphornsuvan, "James D. B. De Bow and the Political Economy of the Old South" (Ph.D. diss., State University of New York at Binghamton, 1990). For aspects of the debate over industrialization especially pertinent here see my *The Political Economy of Slavery: Studies in the Economy and Society of the Slave South* (2nd ed.; Middletown, Conn.: Wesleyan University Press, 1989), pp. 180–239.

17. Henry Hughes, *Treatise on Sociology, Theoretical and Practical* (New York: Negro Universities Press, 1968 [1854]), p. 47. A first-rate study of Hughes has long been needed and has finally arrived. See Douglas Ambrose, "'The Man for Times Coming': The Life and Thought of Henry Hughes" (Ph.D. dissertation, State University of New York at Binghamton, 1991).

18. See Elizabeth Fox-Genovese, "Property and Patriarchy in Classical Bourgeois Political Theory," *Radical History Review*, 4 (1977), 5–29.

19. McCord's economic and social views are analyzed in Fox-Genovese, *Within the Plantation Household*, esp. ch. 5.

20. Eugene D. Genovese and Elizabeth Fox-Genovese, "Slavery, Economic Development, and the Law: The Dilemma of Southern Political Economists, 1800–1860," *Washington and Lee Law Review*, 41 (1984), 1–29.

21. Palmer, *Life and Letters of Thornwell*, pp. 482–483. For Thornwell's views on millennialism see esp., Morton H. Smith, *Studies in Southern Presbyterian Theology* (Philipsburg, N.J.: Presbyterian and Reformed Publishing Co., 1987), pp. 180–181.

22. Cobb, *Law of Negro Slavery*, p. 283.

23. Bell Irwin Wiley, "The Movement to Humanize the Institution of Slavery During the Confederacy," *Emory University Quarterly*, 5 (1949), 207–220. Perhaps the most powerful contemporary statement was Calvin H. Wiley, *Scriptural Views of National Trials* (Greensboro, N.C.: Sterling, Campbell, and Albright, 1863). The call for reform as a matter of realizing the slaveholders' duty to God had deep antebellum roots and reverberated through the religious press and the writings of jurists and others.

24. William W. Freehling has forcefully demonstrated the catastrophic consequences that followed the slaveholders' attacks on civil rights in the North. See especially his lengthy analysis of the struggle over the Gag Rule in *Road to Disunion: Secessionists at Bay*, pp. 287–352.

25. Clement Eaton, *The Freedom-of-Thought Struggle in the Old South* (Rev. and enl. ed.; New York: Harper & Row, 1964).

26. Simms, *Views and Reviews in American Literature: History and Fiction*, ed. C. Hugh Holman (Cambridge, Mass.: The Belknap Press of Harvard University Press, 1962), pp. 36–38.

27. As quoted in Stanford M. Lyman, ed., *Selected Writings of Henry Hughes: Antebellum Southerner, Slavocrat, Sociologist* (Jackson: University Press of Mississippi, 1985), p. xiii.

28. Simms to William Alfred Jones, June 10, 1851, in Simms, *Letters*, V, 414.

29. Simms to Hammond, March 27, 1858; Simms to Lawson, March 21, 1860 — in Simms, *Letters*, IV, 42, 208. See "The Morals of Slavery," 1837, as reprinted in *The Pro-Slavery Argument, as Maintained by the Most Distinguished Writers of the Southern States, Containing the Several Essays, on the Subject, of Chancellor Harper, Governor Hammond, Dr. Simms, and Professor Dew* (Philadelphia: Lippincott, Grambo, & Co., 1853), pp. 181–285.

30. On Wilde, see Edward L. Tucker, *Richard Henry Wilde: His Life and Selected Poems* (Athens: University of Georgia Press, 1966). For the report of Byron's praise see Thomas Gamble, *Savannah Duels and Duellists, 1733–1877* (Savannah, Ga.: Review Publishing and Printing Co., 1974), p. 153. Anthony Barclay, a classical scholar and British consul at Havana, said that "My Life is Like the Summer Rose" established Wilde's international fame. On Chivers see Charles Henry Watts II, *Thomas Holley Chivers: His Literary Career and His Poetry* (Athens: University of Georgia Press, 1956); Emma Lester Chose and Lois Ferry Parks,

eds., *The Complete Works of Thomas Holley Chivers* (Providence, R.I.: Brown University Press, 1957). See also F. M. Garrett, *Atlanta and Environs: A Chronicle of Its People and Events* (Athens: University of Georgia Press, 1954), I, 442–44; Meade Minnigerode, *The Fabulous Forties, 1840–1850: A Presentation of Private Life* (New York: G. P. Putnam's Sons, 1924), pp. 116–119.

31. See J. E. D. Shipp, *Giant Days; or, The Life and Times of William H. Crawford* (Americus, Ga.: Southern Printers, 1909), p. 193 for the text of Wilde's letter.

32. Watts, *Chivers*, p. 190; see also pp. 48–53 and the scattered references to Chivers's newspaper articles.

33. For an introduction to Grayson and Timrod in the intellectual context of Charleston see David Moltke-Hansen's splendid survey, "The Expansion of Intellectual Life: A Prospectus," ch. 1 of O'Brien and Moltke-Hansen, eds., *Intellectual Life in Antebellum Charleston*, pp. 3–44; and Richard J. Calhoun, "William J. Grayson: Autobiographer," in Calhoun, ed., *Witness to Sorrow: The Antebellum Autobiography of William J. Grayson* (Columbia: University of South Carolina Press, 1990), pp. 1–34. For contrasting interpretations of Timrod's ideology see Rubin, *Edge of the Swamp*, pp. 190–225; and Lewis P. Simpson, "The South's Reaction to Modernism," in Louis D. Rubin, Jr., and C. Hugh Holman, eds., *Southern Literary Study: Problems and Possibilities* (Chapel Hill: University of North Carolina Press, 1975), pp. 61–64; and Simpson, *Dispossessed Garden*, pp. 81–82. On Timrod, whose poetry was highly praised in the North by Whittier and Emerson, among others, see also Edd Winfield Parks, ed., *The Essays of Henry Timrod* (Athens: University of Georgia Press, 1942), esp. Parks's Introduction, pp. 26–29, and Timrod's "Literature in the South," pp. 83–102.

34. Timrod, "Ethnogenesis," in Paul H. Hayne, ed., *The Poems of Henry Timrod* (New York: E. J. Hale & Son, 1873), pp. 103–104.

35. J. S. Morris, *Impromptu Lines* (Port Gibson, Miss.: Office of the Daily Reveille, 1859). That Oakland College had the poem published is especially noteworthy since it was regarded locally as a hotbed of unionism.

36. Grayson, *Hireling and Slave, Chicora, and Other Poems* (Charleston, S.C.: Russell & Jones, 1858). See also Grayson, "The Dual Form of Labor," *DeBow's Review*, 28 (1860), 48–66.

37. Grayson, as quoted in William Sumner Jenkins, *Pro-Slavery Thought in the Old South* (Gloucester, Mass.: Peter Smith, 1960), p. 303.

3

Adventurism and Paralysis

The dilemma inherent in the formula of progress through freedom based on slavery emerged with full force in the thought of William H. Trescot and James Henry Hammond, two intellectually powerful South Carolinians whose historical and political writing may serve as well as any alternative to elucidate the formula, its contradictions, and the political impasse into which it led.

"The leading fact in modern history is — to borrow a philosophical phrase almost generalized into common use — its progress by antagonisms." So wrote Trescot in the opening pages of his extraordinary book *The Diplomacy of the Revolution*. Every historical age, he continued, "has a general tendency, a uniform character, and a precise result, yet all this will have been attained by the conflict of opposing national interests; and in each nation the governing interest will have been nurtured through the conduct of opposing parties."[1] Trescot's interpretation of history rested on three ideas: progress was discernible in human affairs; national struggles propel that progress; and social struggles determine the internal character of the antagonistic nations.

Much of Trescot's thought, especially that portion he chose to expose in *The Diplomacy of the Revolution*, could readily be assimilated to transatlantic conservatism, as well as the more politically cautious strands of political and economic liberalism. Not only the analyses but the temper of Trescot's book appealed to Edward Everett and other prominent Yankees and provided him with a passport to the State Department. Trescot scored his literary coup through a simple act of prudence: He concentrated on an elaboration of the part of his historical interpretation that concerned international antagonisms and restricted the part that concerned internal social antagonisms to a broadly conservative attack on left-wing radicalism. He further appealed to a wide spectrum of liberal as well as conservative opinion by insisting that the American Revolution was an epoch-making national but not social or ideological event. American independence, wrote Trescot, did indeed open a new era in history, but, in an implicit attack on Thomas Paine and other radical democrats, he insisted that that era was new because of the introduction of "a new power, but not a new principle." The United States' successful claim to admission into the community of nations was "eminently a conservative one, implying a distinct recognition of the justice of the system into which they desired to enter."[2]

Trescot stressed the importance of international law, which had arisen in Europe to keep national antagonisms within civilized limits, and he gave full credit to the monarchies that made both the law and its extension to America possible. After the American Revolution, he wrote, "The United States took their place in the world as the inventors of no new political doctrine, as the disturbers of no old political rights. . . . Republics were not novelties even in the European system." The great practical effect of the entrance of the United States into the European system of nations was "simply, that in obedience to that law of progress which governs all growth, the balance of power must henceforth be adjusted for a wide sphere, for more momentous interests, and for greater ends."[3]

There were few monarchists among the slaveholders of the Old South, although more than yet noticed. Trescot was not among their number, notwithstanding his deep respect for the statesmanship of the European monarchies and his conviction that many peoples could not sustain republican institutions. He had a lot of company in the South, where an increasing number of prominent and ordinary slaveholders were expressing doubts that the French, among other Europeans, deserved or could maintain republican institutions and the freedom that they sustained.[4] Trescot's own forthright republicanism attested to his conviction that the greater freedom made possible by a republic constituted a source of national strength. A neo-Federalist Whig, Trescot stood close to Fitzhugh and Hughes in favoring a strong government and opposing laissez-faire. He condemned state rights and argued that slavery required considerable centralization of political power to protect its "feudal necessities." Scoffing at Calhoun as well as Jefferson, Trescot called for secession not because the North was centralizing power but because it was centralizing it in opposition to the slaveholding interest.[5]

In a letter to James Henley Thornwell, Trescot praised Motley's history of the Dutch Republic for offering the finest "genuine illustration of the American mind in the field of history." Motley, he explained, stands "upon the vantage ground of our republican institutions and the work goes to prove what I have always maintained, that a true philosophical history of modern Europe can be written only by a highly cultivated and conscientious American."[6] In this way Trescot joined the myriad of southern writers who, down to Allen Tate and the Agrarians, have seen the United States as heir to the best in the Christian heritage of the West and have seen the South as the region that has proven worthy since the North capitulated to infidelity, radical democracy, and moral decadence.

Trescot consistently argued for a republicanism based upon an aristocracy that alone could sustain a proper measure of internal democracy. As Trescot wrote to William Porcher Miles in 1859, the slaveocracy brought aristocratic features with its rule and for just that reason could no longer remain in the Union.[7] Sensitive to the wide variations in the historical experience of diverse peoples, he did not hold up his preferred kind of republicanism as a model for the world, but he did ground historical progress in the development of specific nations. As David Moltke-Hansen trenchantly observes, "Complicating his own vision of history as linear movement was his belief that individual nations, and the races and classes composing them, have life cycles. They are born, develop, flourish, weaken, wither, and finally are absorbed by new and aggressively developing competitors."[8]

From this context emerge the implications of Trescot's assignment of a great historical future for the United States, or rather for the southern confederacy it was extruding. He identified slavery as the foundation of the aristocratic republican freedom that provided the driving force for progress in the modern world, and he identified the South as the embodiment of the social and political virtues that had raised the Christian West astride the world. In *The Diplomacy of the Revolution* he had no need to dwell on the social basis of the emergence and subsequent renting of the new republic. But in other writings of the early 1850s he had to turn his attention to that social basis. In so doing, he picked up the relay from Dew while transforming Dew's steadily less plausible case for the Union into a strong case for recognition of an emerging southern nation.

The Diplomacy of the Revolution, read in isolation, as northerners seem to have read it, carried an implicit plea to the northern bourgeoisie to reassess its own position and to turn toward an alliance with the southern slaveholders against lower-class radicalism. Yet on July 4, 1850, shortly before the publication of his history, Trescot laid his secessionist cards on the table in a speech in Beaufort, S.C., which he revised and published in pamphlet form as *The Position and Course of the South.*[9] Had it been read and taken seriously in the North, Trescot might not have been wooed by the State Department and have risen to become acting secretary of state in the Buchanan administration. For Trescot, scorning to hide his views, did not rest with an attack on the antislavery attitudes that were bursting forth in the North. He attacked northern society itself for its free-labor social relations.

Trescot, no mere propagandist or sectional hothead, as-

sumed responsibility for making the case for the national rights of
the southern people, much as he had done retrospectively for the
rights of the American people in the revolutionary era. He had
positioned himself well to add the social dimension to the political and constitutional dimensions of the impending struggle for
power. At first glance, the opposite might appear true. Since
Trescot denied the claims of Paine and the radical democrats for a
social interpretation of the American Revolution, he might be
expected to have restricted his discussion to political and constitutional issues, but he could not do so without doing violence
to the principles that informed his interpretation of history and
his worldview.

As an American diplomat as well as a historian, Trescot had
always advocated the rule of law in international affairs. He
viewed that rule as the framework for the coexistence of rival
ideologies and social systems within a transatlantic Christian
civilization. Nations had the right to self-determination and the
right to defend their national-state interests. They also had another right, which qualified the first on the basis of the second —
the right to intervene in the internal affairs of any nation that was
posing a threat to the stability of the world order. Nations could
claim the right to self-determination only so long as their internal
policies and social struggles did not threaten to spill over into an
attack on the property rights and social, economic, and political
systems of other nations.

The United States had arisen on the basis of a political compromise between two sectionally based social systems, and its
claims to embrace a single nationality rested upon each section's
scrupulous adherence to the terms of the constitutional compromise. As that adherence and mutual respect ebbed, and as the
North launched its aggression against the southern system, two
distinct nationalities began to emerge. The claims for a southern
confederacy thereby constituted an analogue to the previous
claims of the thirteen colonies against Great Britain, not because
the South had a discrete social system but because its constitutional and political rights were being violated. By seceding from

the Union, the South would be petitioning for entrance into Christendom's system of national states but would not be threatening the international status quo. The South, like the original thirteen states, was following an eminently conservative course to secession.

Trescot considered the North socially, not merely politically, aggressive and a threat to international law and comity. In effect, he sought to establish a theoretical and legal basis for European intervention to sustain the rights of the South in case of war. Thus he had to demonstrate the socially radical and internationally subversive character of the northern attack on the South. In *The Position and Course of the South*, Trescot warmed up with ten pages of legal and constitutional argument and then struck hard on the underlying social question. Unfortunately for his cause, he had to risk irritating the Europeans he sought as allies by criticizing the social system they shared with the North. "Look for a moment," he began, "at the condition of the operatives of England and France. In both the population is free, labour and capital are politically equal; while, in fact, capital tyrannizes over labour with selfish power, holding labour to its terrible bond — the obligation a life of barely sustained toil — the penalty death by starvation."[10]

Trescot read Henry Mayhew, among other critics of British society, and, in various speeches and publications, reacted with disgust to the account of the degradation of the laboring classes. "They live — they work — they die," he cried. "When they fall, they fall as in battle, and the ranks of the innumerable army of workmen close and trample over them, no heart to pity and no time to mourn."[11] He helped finance publication and distribution of Grayson's "The Hireling and the Slave" to expose the horrors of capitalist exploitation and the benefits of slavery. He denounced the lack of moral obligation between capital and labor and warned that the laboring classes, which understood political theory only in its practical results, would "rebel against the powers that be."[12]

The English Chartists, Trescot noted in *The Position and*

Course of the South, were calling for equal representation and an end to the aristocratic institutions that were increasingly being exposed as bastions of entrenched capital. The Chartists were demanding, "logically enough, we must say, that the nation should abandon the palpable inconsistency of free labour and a privileged class." He found the logic of the French socialists "still stricter and more unscrupulous" in its demonstration "that if labour and capital are equal in principle, they should be equal in practice, and that all property is theft." Reason and history confirm, he added, that labor would rebel against politically entrenched class power, but it could not put an end to social stratification and the domination of property.

Trescot elaborated: The divinely inspired Hebrew commonwealth, the Greek states, the Roman Empire all underwent political upheavals but did not suffer the overthrow of their servile social relations. "In the ancient world, the relation of labour and capital took the shape of slavery, and what disturbances did it work? In the modern world, it has taken the shape of service, and what civil commotion, what parliamentary perplexity has it not wrought?" Concluding his review of the deepening crisis of bourgeois social relations, he announced, "We have arrived at the great contradiction between the institutions of the North and South."

Trescot thereupon laid out the slaveholders' claims to having the superior social system. The South had stratified and harmonious social relations, while the North, wallowing in an illusion of equality, had brutally antagonistic and oppressive social relations. "Can a more violent contrast be imagined?" Trescot contrasted the ominous political power of the laboring, oppressed, and swelling majority in the North with the political impotence of a contented and subordinated class of slaves in the South, adding, "It requires but ordinary sagacity to see that this difference of relation between labour and capital, necessitates for the North and South the development of two individual and inconsistent systems both of representation and taxation."

After elaborating that incompatibility in the familiar southern manner, Trescot continued, "And here it may be remarked that, wherever labour and capital have been recognized as theoretically equal, society has been forced in self-preservation, to the creation of artificial privileged classes. Equality of rights and privileges can, in the nature of things, exist only where the participants of political power form a separate class." At this point he introduced the race question to suggest that class relations could be much more easily adjusted and pacified when they followed racial lines. As for the North, where the white race was divided by class, the conditions that had long mediated class relations were "fast vanishing" and an all-out class war was in the making. Trescot had to take the plunge into the social question if he were going to construct a coherent analysis consistent with his historical and political framework. And with a host of other prominent southerners, he expected the transatlantic bourgeoisies to move toward the restoration of some form of personal servitude for the laboring classes of their own countries.

Trescot tried to minimize the risk of offending conservative opinion outside the South. In *The Diplomacy of the Revolution*, he commended the European monarchies for having developed a system of international law based upon the principle of mutual toleration of different political and social systems. Even in *The Position and Course of the South*, he denounced the North not so much for maintaining a reprehensible social system as for trying to solve its internal problems by aggression against the rival system it was constitutionally bound to tolerate and respect. And he denounced the North for trumpeting a radical-democratic and egalitarian ideology that breathed a sense of international mission and thereby threatened all conservative regimes, bourgeois included, and that displayed a flagrant contempt for the rule of law. Thus Trescot cast the South as an emerging nation that adhered to principles and policies compatible with Europe's dominant interests. And thus he cast the North not as another rising bourgeois power but as the new center of the dreaded Jacobin challenge to international law and social order.

Only one conclusion followed from Trescot's analysis, although he never fully articulated it. Perhaps like Dew, he wisely meant to leave room for human ingenuity in devising surprising solutions to great problems. His analysis paralleled that of such outstanding social and political theorists as Dew, Calhoun, Fitzhugh, Holmes, and Hammond and such outstanding divines as Thornwell, Dabney, Stringfellow, Ross, and Smith in viewing the North and Europe as facing social convulsion and the unraveling of their bourgeois socioeconomic and political systems. But more sharply than most others, he envisioned the superior slave system of the South as the guarantor of a southern confederacy's own rise to world power. For unless Europe and the North heeded southern advice, which swelled to massive proportions during the 1850s, and reinstituted some form of personal servitude for its laboring classes, only the South would be able to preserve the political and economic freedom of a ruling class capable of leading a great nation in the perpetual struggle among contending nations and peoples. National "antagonisms" propelled human progress, and the strength and weakness of nations depended upon a stable outcome of the internal struggles inherent in their class relations.

Trescot never worked out, as Dew had done, the specific role of freedom in the generation of national power. But at every point his historical analysis is compatible with Dew's. Thus, in his spirited and penetrating essay on the origins of the Crimean War, Trescot announced: "The first principle of life is progress," and he linked progress to English freedom. While taking the side of Russia in the immediate encounter, he wrote, "We would not have the power of England positively diminished one iota; for she has played a great and noble part in the world's history. She has been the foster-mother of commerce, . . . and in her living language were uttered the first broken sentences of constitutional liberty."[13] Trescot's several celebrations of the advantages of American republicanism implicitly restated Dew's position. And for Trescot, as for Dew and the principal southern theorists of the 1840s and 1850s, republican freedom, especially under conditions of industrial and technological progress, depended upon the en-slavement of the laboring classes and, more broadly, upon a clearly elaborated division of society by class to sustain a republi-can polity.[14]

One danger Trescot does not seem to have anticipated. What if the South seceded, as he counseled, before the social system of its bourgeois rivals unraveled? Whatever the supposed beauties of republican freedom under slavery, all signs pointed toward the enormous military advantage attendant upon the eco-nomic power of the free-labor system, however high its social cost. Indeed, if the social system of Western Europe was unravel-ing and that of the North was destined to follow suit, did not good sense dictate, as the proslavery southern unionists pleaded, that the South remain in the Union and bide its time, rather than risk war with a nation palpably superior in economic might?[15]

It is hard to believe that Trescot, of all people, did not have these questions in mind as he wrote letters and notes in which he explored political possibilities. His interpretation of history left much room for human action, and if the risks ran high, so did the stakes. Vigorous peoples had defied the odds before and won. Secession might, as the unionists cried, be adventurist. But for Trescot, when national existence became the stakes, a great peo-ple had to assert itself, even to the point of playing *va banque*.

James Henry Hammond had his doubts. For three decades he brooded over the myth and reality of progress, the course of Western civilization, and the destiny of southern slave society. His struggle to master the ideological contradictions and their central dilemma plunged him into a long quarrel with himself, which laid bare the most dangerous tensions in the slaveholders' worldview. Hammond rose from middling origins to become a large and successful planter, congressman, governor, United States senator, and frustrated heir-apparent to the mantle of the great Calhoun. He deserved his reputation for intellectual power, much as he deserved his reputation for moral laxity, self-indulgence, self-pity, and the abuse of the women in his life.

Whatever may be said of his personal behavior, the quality of his intellect cannot fairly be questioned.[16]

Hammond began his career on Calhoun's right flank, pushing hard for radical state action even if it meant secession. In the 1850s, after Calhoun's death, he moderated his views considerably, braving the ire of his constituents by plunging into a fruitless effort to prevent what he regarded as a premature and therefore potentially suicidal secession. Thus he retreated from an espousal of his long-sought goal of a separate southern nation at the very moment the dying Calhoun was reluctantly and bitterly accepting it. It were as if the death of the father stripped the rebellious son of his *raison d'être*. In the end, Hammond reluctantly joined his fellow senator, James Chesnut, in resigning his seat and in returning to South Carolina to contribute, as best he might, to the attempt to build a new nation. By then he was a spent man who could do little except carp at the inadequacies of the Confederate war effort. In retrospect, his death during the war seems an anticlimax to a life at once brilliant and absurd, glorious and pitiful, triumphant and ill-spent.

A speech by the youthful Hammond to the U. S. House of Representatives in 1836 electrified the South and raised him to immediate prominence. Admirers predicted great things for him, including perhaps the presidency of the United States. Almost immediately his career wavered, much as it did in the wake of his governorship in the 1840s, and again in the 1850s, when he seemed politically paralyzed by South Carolina's course to secession. In the first instance he collapsed with intestinal troubles that even then aroused suspicions of mental problems. He left Congress and sailed for Europe to regain his health. In the second instance he provoked Wade Hampton, his wife's powerful kinsman, and no few others into sending him into the political wilderness. Incredibly, Hammond had whiled away his leisure hours in the governor's mansion in sexual dalliance with Hampton's four teen-age daughters, that is, with his own nieces. Fortunately for Hammond, Hampton had a principled, if for a South Carolinian unusual, opposition to dueling and the settling of personal scores by violence, and he proved strong enough to prevent his chivalrous young relatives from drawing their pistols on the field of honor or in the streets of Columbia. In the third instance Hammond, having finally reentered the political lists, proved incapable of decisive action of any kind.

That Hammond's psyche played havoc with his career should be obvious. It would be hard to find a clearer case of a man who craved power and yet feared to wield it — except over his family and slaves, whom he tried to rule with an iron hand. This fear of political power does not seem typical of the slaveholders. Hence it is tempting to analyze his ideological and political course as a problem in psychology, and his mental state undoubtedly accounts for some of his inconsistencies and especially for his hesitations. Yet any such psychological analysis would risk considerable injustice to a man who, whatever his personal failings, normally thought clearly and deeply about the world. More dangerously, it would risk losing sight of the extent to which those inconsistencies and hesitations faithfully reflected the dilemmas inherent in the slaveholders' worldview. And if it be argued, however speculatively, that Hammond's personal crises heightened his understanding of those dilemmas and hesitations, so be it.

Hammond rose in the House of Representatives determined to provoke a confrontation over the reception of abolitionist petitions. He refused to apologize for slavery or restrict himself to constitutional ground. Even then, with most of his peers still cautious about debating the larger implications of the slavery question, he quickly seized the high ground. The only reason, he charged, that the North had given up slavery — the only reason that Britain and continental Europe had given up villeinage and serfdom — was that free labor had proven cheaper than servile labor. He attributed the different course of the South to the effects of climate and to the international effects of the industrial revolution, and he argued that the South needed slave labor to survive in the competitive world into which it had been catapulted. So far he had invoked, if belligerently, familiar arguments, but he proceeded in a different vein: "Sir, I do firmly believe that domestic slavery regulated as ours is produces the highest toned, the purest, best organization of society that has ever existed on the face of the earth."[17]

In the course of his inflammatory yet thoughtful speech, Hammond presented his views on the progress and prospects of the human race. We have reached, he began, a new era in civilization, for the man of the nineteenth century differs markedly from the man of the eighteenth. In an obvious reference to the effects of industrialization, he suggested that civilized man had undergone deeper change during the last half century or so than he had previously undergone since the time of Charlemagne. A vast increase in knowledge was forging a new material world, a new moral climate, and a new kind of man. With mixed feelings he referred to the overthrow of kings and hierarchies and the decline of the power of the clergy in the wake of "that terrible tragedy, the French Revolution, which was confessedly brought about by the writings of the great philosophers of France." He elaborated: "Since that period, man appears no longer to be the being that he was. His moral nature seems to have been changed as by some sudden revelation from the lips of the Almighty."[18]

Hammond took full account of the changes wrought by steampower and other advances in technology: "In one word, we have reached a period when physical impossibilities are no longer spoken of." But social relations, not economic development per se, engaged his primary attention and invited a warning: "During the period of this mighty change, the great struggle between the rulers and the ruled has been carried on with corresponding vigor." The very expression "the people" now was conjuring up "the MOB – THE SANS CULOTTES." The Jeffersonian silliness about equality, paraded in the Declaration of Independence, now has become the rallying cry of the "ignorant, uneducated, semibarbarous mass which swarms and starves upon the face of Europe!"[19]

The abolitionists, he observed, identify the southern slaveholders with the old aristocracies. Hammond agreed: "In this they are right. I accept the terms. *It is a government of the best,* combining all the advantages, and possessing but few of the disadvantages of the aristocracy of the old world. . . . Slavery does indeed create an aristocracy— an aristocracy of talents, of virtues, of generosity and courage. In a slave country *every freeman* is an aristocrat." Hammond closed by warning that sans-cullottism was rising in New England and spreading westward. At this point he announced his conviction that southern slavery had produced the best society yet known to man.[20] Hammond's trip to Europe reinforced his view. Upon returning in 1837, he compared the southern planters with the European nobles as their respective societies' embodiment of honor and independence, and he concluded, "Both stand at the head of society and politics."[21]

The ambivalence toward material progress and the revolution in knowledge that Hammond expressed in that early speech accompanied him through life. Such progress was breathtaking, wonderful, a joy to behold and participate in. And it was leading to a social catastrophe. His trip to Europe confirmed his conviction that slavery alone could prevent the worst. In his letters he denounced the democratic despotism that universal suffrage was opening the way to and predicted increasing revolutionary violence against a social system that could not take care of the mass of its people. "The next cycle of barbarism" he wrote, "will be consummated by overturning all existing establishment. . . . A Republican Government develops more fully than any other the energy of its people and calls into exercise the character and talents of the underclasses beyond any other political organization." Had, then, Europe made a monarchist of him? Not at all. He never doubted that a republic would be preferable to a monarchy, as long as it rested on slavery.[22]

Some years later Hammond crisply replied to an antislavery declaration of the Free Church of Glasgow, Scotland. Wasting no time on apologetics, he took the offensive. We have, he said, read the Parliamentary Reports on labor conditions in Britain and have verified them with our own eyes. The Reports show that our slaves, among other advantages, get much more to eat, especially meat and breadstuffs, than your agricultural laborers, and the same might be said in a comparison of our slaves' diet with that of the peasants of France. Your laborers are certainly free — free to beg, steal, and starve.[23]

The mid 1840s, when Hammond answered the Free Church of Glasgow, proved a busy time for him, intellectually as well as politically. The Bluffton Movement, in which he participated, mounted an unsuccessful challenge to Calhoun's presumed political moderation, and Hammond became unusually active in formulating and disseminating advanced proslavery views. No one could have been surprised when, in his gubernatorial message to the state legislature, he announced that South Carolina's patience with the Union was not inexhaustible. As he often did, he took the opportunity to deliver a lecture on the broad significance of slavery for the modern world. South Carolina, he insisted, above all other states supported the Union, for its social relations dictated a conservative position: "There is no State which has less to gain by anarchy and revolution, or that is less disposed to plunge into them wantonly. Neither her fundamental institutions, nor her legislation betray a love of change." He did not have to remind the legislators that South Carolina, more than any other state, had successfully resisted the democratic reforms that had been sweeping the nation.[24]

In the early months of 1844, Hammond developed his thought in two published and widely circulated letters to Thomas Clarkson, the grand old man of the British antislavery movement. Hammond acquitted himself well and drew high praise from fellow southerners for his able polemics. Able or no, the polemics included some sleight of hand. "If you were to ask me whether I am an advocate of slavery in the abstract," he wrote, "I should probably answer, that I am not, according to my understanding of the question. I do not like to deal in abstractions." James Henry

Hammond dealt with the practical affairs of mankind. Now, Hammond knew perfectly well that the question concerned not philosophical abstractions but the specific issue of slavery abstracted from immediate circumstance, especially the matter of race. He compounded his disingenuousness by adding that he was "no more in favor of slavery in the abstract, than I am of poverty, disease, deformity, idiocy, or any other inequality in the condition of the human family."[25]

Here, Hammond was clearly invoking the Christian doctrine of the social as well as personal consequences of the fall of man, but he fell into bad faith or at least into the questionable theology that was being advanced by some notable southern divines. For while slavery might be lumped with poverty or disease as a misfortune attributable to the consequences of original sin, it differed fundamentally — much as the more general principle of social hierarchy did — in constituting a positive restraint designed to protect man against his own depraved nature. The question therefore reduced to acceptance or rejection of slavery as a morally acceptable device for checking the sinful impulses of man in his fallen state. And since Hammond unequivocally deemed slavery morally acceptable and indeed socially necessary, he in effect did endorse the abstract principle of slavery. His invocation of disease and idiocy as lamentable but unavoidable consequences of man's fate — as burdens to be borne but hardly endorsed — at best obfuscated the issue.

Hammond thereupon proceeded to do the very thing he supposedly scorned to do. He endorsed slavery in the abstract. Bowing to convention and implicitly recognizing the religious convictions of his own people as well as of Clarkson and the abolitionists, he opened with a lengthy review of the scriptural teachings on slavery. Not content with scriptural sanction for slavery as one possible status in a necessarily stratified society, he argued that the Apostles regarded slavery "as an *established* as well as *inevitable condition of human society.*" Hammond then reiterated his longstanding arguments on the incompatibility of republican government with the social conditions of Europe and the North and insisted that only the United States, among the great nations of the West, did not need immense standing armies to overawe the laboring classes. But the North's turn would come: "Nor will it be long before the *'Free States'* of the Union will be compelled to introduce the same expensive machinery to preserve order among their 'free and equal' citizens."[26]

In contrast, Hammond held up the South as a more genuinely Christian society. "Slaveholders," he wrote, "are responsible to the world for the humane treatment of their fellow human-beings whom God has placed in their hands. . . . Every man in independent circumstances, all the world over, and every Government, is to the same extent responsible to the whole human family for the condition of the poor and laboring classes in their own country." Yet, he charged, your society shamelessly degrades, morally and physically, its "fellow citizens," not merely "fellow human beings." You pay wages on which your laborers subsist barely if at all, whereas we, without technically paying any wages at all, provide a substantially better life for ours.[27]

As for slavery in the abstract, the subject he had scorned to discuss while he in fact discussed it, he could hardly have been clearer. Concluding his indictment of the free labor system, he reiterated, "Slavery is an established and inevitable condition to human society. I do not speak of the *name*, but of the *fact*." And for those slow to understand, he added, "The fact cannot be denied, that the mere laborer is now, and always has been, everywhere that barbarism has ceased, enslaved."[28]

Thus Hammond's famous "Cotton Is King" speech to the United States Senate in March 1858, which offered the mudsill theory, recapitulated doctrines he had been advancing for two decades. The speech enraged northerners for its flamboyant declaration, "No, you dare not make war on cotton. No power on earth dares to make war upon it. Cotton *Is* king." More ominously, it enraged northerners by its condemnation of the northern and its celebration of the southern social system. The many workers who learned of that speech and rallied to Lincoln in 1860 loudly shouted that they would neither forget nor forgive. "The greatest strength of the South," Hammond began, "arises from the harmony of her political and social institutions. This harmony gives her a frame of society, the best in the world, and an extent of political freedom, combined with entire security, such as no other people ever enjoyed upon the face of the earth."[29] He then dropped the hammer. Insisting, as he had to Clarkson, that the North had a class of laborers who were slaves in everything except name and in the lack of protection afforded by southern slavery, he summed up:

> In all social systems there must be a class to do the menial duties, to perform the drudgery of life. That is, a class requiring but a low order of intellect and but little skill. Its requisites are vigor, docility, fidelity. Such a class you must have, or you would not have that other class which leads progress, civilization, and refinement. It constitutes the very mud-sill of society and political government; and you might as well attempt to build a house in the air, as to build either the one or the other, except on this mud-sill. Fortunately for the South, she found a race adapted to that purpose to her hand.[30]

Clyde Wilson has suggestively interpreted Hammond's mudsill metaphor as a bid for the favor of the northern working class. "Read in context," Wilson writes, "the statement may be more reasonably seen as one of sympathetic alliance with the labor of the North. It is the capitalists that Hammond regards as his enemy and undertakes to insult."[31] As Wilson well knows, Calhoun had more than once tested those waters. So why not Hammond?

Hammond doubtless kept an eye on such an alliance — a kind of updated version of Van Buren's old alliance of "planters and plain republicans" — but political realities also forced him to keep an eye on the alternative occasionally offered by Fitzhugh: an alliance of slaveholders with conservative northern capitalists who were beginning to worry about working-class insurgency. Hammond had no way out. However much he sympathized, or claimed to sympathize, with the plight of northern labor, he could hardly endorse a working-class program for the North. His social conservatism and interpretation of political economy forbade it.

Recall that Hammond had attributed the decline of slavery and serfdom in Europe and the North to the bourgeoisie's ability to profit from the laws of political economy. That is, economic development had rendered free labor cheaper and more easily exploited than servile labor. The North, he argued, was increasingly confronting a struggle between rapacious capitalists, flushed with an unprecedented accumulation of capital, and a working class that faced immiseration. Like Dew, Calhoun, Fitzhugh, and every other southern theorist, including his old mentor Thomas Cooper, Hammond dismissed the idea of socialism or working-class government as an impossibility, but he recognized the socialist movement as a threat to civilization and an invitation to anarchy and despotism. Hence Wilson's shrewd reading of Hammond's intent illuminates political tactics, not strategy, much less principle.

By Hammond's own logic the civilized, Christian, practical solution to the social question in the bourgeois countries could only be found in slavery. He did suggest that the North and other countries should and would resort to African slaves where feasible, but he does not appear to have believed that that feasibility could extend far enough to solve the problem at hand. Rather, for him as for the professed supporters of slavery in the abstract, the logic of the argument pointed toward the restoration of some form of slavery or industrial servitude as the necessary condition of the laboring classes of all races. He had to know that no political alliance could be forged on such terms, which could not even be presented for serious political discussion.[32]

How, then, did Hammond evaluate the idea of progress and the fate of the modern world? He discussed these matters in his

first letter to Clarkson and, five years later, in an oration to the
students of South Carolina College. He wrote Clarkson:

> The events of the last three-quarters of a century appear to
> have revolutionized the human mind. Enterprise and ambi-
> tion are only limited in their purposes by the horizon of the
> imagination It is a transcendental era. In philosophy, re-
> ligion, government, science, arts, commerce, nothing that
> has been is to be allowed to be. Conservatism in any form is
> scoffed at. The slightest taint of it is fatal. Where will this
> end?[33]

Hammond offered a maxim: "The best criterion of the future
is the past." He launched into another assault on the French
Revolution and all its works and hopefully suggested, "Mankind,
still horror-stricken by the catastrophe of France, have shrunk
from rash experiments upon social systems." But, he complained,
referring to the West Indian emancipation and other events the
world over, the madness goes on and now threatens the South and
all civilization. He appealed to Clarkson, or more likely, through
these letters destined for publication, to his fellow southerners:
"For our own sake, and for the sake of those infatuated men who
are madly driving on the conflagration; for the sake of human
nature, we are called on to strain every nerve to arrest it."[34]

When Hammond returned to the theme in 1849 in the oration delivered before the two student societies of South Carolina
College, he resumed his attack on the cult of progress in a manner
that betrayed no small admiration for the substance of the progress he had long been attacking. He knew he would be speaking
not only to students who represented the flower of the rising
generation, but to the politically powerful intellectual elite of his
state. He knew that the occasion required his best effort and that
he had better choose his words carefully. The pros and cons of
progress furnished his theme, and he began by reviewing the
remarkable developments in communications and transportation
and the discoveries and advances in science and art.

The slashing sarcasm of his letters to Clarkson gave way to a more balanced evaluation. "We are," he noted, "accustomed to regard the age in which we live not only as the most enlightened which the world has known, but one of unprecedented progress."[35] He proceeded to denounce Jeremy Bentham and the utilitarians for slighting the wisdom of the past and to criticize at curious length those who were attributing the modern revolution in scientific knowledge to Francis Bacon. Hammond acknowledged Bacon as "a truly great man" but sought to reduce his stature enough to call into question the doctrines of the utilitarians who claimed his mantle. Possibly too, Hammond intended to bait the Reverend Dr. James Henley Thornwell and Columbia's other Presbyterian divines who doted on Bacon as the great exponent of the inductive method, which, in their view, demonstrated the compatibility of modern science with religious orthodoxy. For while Hammond spared no effort to identify himself with the reigning Christian sensibility, he qualified as neither pious nor orthodox. He nonetheless read theology, as he read much else, and counted himself a believer.

Hammond's appeal to Scripture and Christian revelation came as a pleasant surprise to the divines, who had long and reasonably suspected him of indifference to religion, if not worse. Dr. W. Hooper of North Carolina wrote Thornwell in April 1850 that he was reading the pamphlet version of the speech to the students at South Carolina College. "I thought," Hooper mused, "he was the very impersonation of utilitarianism. Here he is the scorner of it. Again, I thought his excellency was not much of a reader or believer in the Bible. Here he appears a staunch Bible man. I hope he may have a better reason for his attachment than that the Bible has lent him weapons against the abolitionists."[36]

Probably, he intended to reduce Bacon's stature only to the extent of defending the claims of classical learning against a modernist assault that the divines also worried about. He generously praised the contributions of the Italians to learning and, through an appreciation of their efforts during the Renaissance, he worked his way back to the ancients. In particular he hailed Aristotle as the great guide to whom all sound modern political and social theorists were indebted. Antiquity, he insisted, had provided humanity's greatest examples of grand thought and noble deeds. Christianity alone accounts for the difference between ancient and modern civilizations — or so he asserted in what Thornwell and the divines might well have regarded as a less than adequate bow to prevailing sentiments. In any case, Hammond defended his thesis, which even the most critical divines had to applaud, by concluding that scientific methods did not constitute the only source of the expanded knowledge on which modern civilization had arisen.

There is a touch of irony in Hammond's invocation of Bacon's "knowledge is power," for he came close to pronouncing the judgment uttered by Richard Weaver a century later: "The final degradation of the Baconian philosophy is that knowledge becomes power in the service of appetite."[37] Hammond doubtless knew Condorcet's celebrated essay on progress, which advanced knowledge as the foundation of all social and moral progress and concluded that the history of civilization has been the history of enlightenment. Hammond foreshadowed the stinging criticism of J. B. Bury, who observed that Condorcet had failed to see that the progress of knowledge depended upon the stability of institutions.[38] Hammond, in his own terms, warned that, if divorced from wholesome institutions and solid traditions, knowledge could only encourage nihilism. There is no reason to doubt that he intended the irony and that much of his audience understood it.

The decks cleared, Hammond finally got to the main business at hand: "What is most desired by Man is power."[39] He praised Charlemagne for having brought order to feudal Europe but bemoaned the retrogression under his successors, who succumbed to the feudal spirit of the age. Then, in a masterpiece of studied ambiguity, he remarked:

The great experiment of Teutonic Monarchy failed in the hands of his successors, overwhelmed by the Feudal spirit of our ancestors. That spirit had yet to accomplish its mission of consecrating the hereditary principle, on the basis of indefeasible fealty, and compensating protection, from generation to generation, of the rulers and the ruled; and to foster still further, a lofty sense of personal dignity and honor, while it promoted patriotism, social sympathy, learning and religion. It is an invaluable lesson to us — a lesson which even to this day has not been fully learned in Europe — that this same Feudal system — slowly and naturally as it had been builded up, rich as were its fruits, indestructible as seemed the well wrought chain, which, stretching from prince to peasant, and penetrating all the intermediary ranks, bound the whole structure of society in links of solid iron — fell beneath the bloodless blows of a despised *Bourgeoisie*.[40]

Here Hammond was simultaneously expressing admiration and awe, fear and revulsion at the onset of the modern age, but this time he named the culprit — "a despised *Bourgeoisie*." After obscurely referring to two centuries of fanaticism and the crushing of chivalry, he continued, "Philosophy and letters, inventions and discoveries, manufactures and trade, sound governments and the refining arts, all advanced side by side, in the great march of progress. Religion lagged behind." He maintained that religion had nonetheless influenced the affairs of men more than all other causes combined, and he cited the Reformation as the most influential event since the advent of Christianity. At that point he might have been expected to join the issue he had been hinting at — the decline of religion, morals, and virtue in the wake of the enormous progress in science and material life. Instead, he trailed off into some less than helpful remarks about the Wars of Religion and the subsequent acceptance of toleration.

For while the irreligion and moral decay of the modern world caused his heart to rebel, the knowledge that accounted for the declension fascinated his brain. He emphatically denied that the primary source of progress lay in the accumulation of wealth, and he seized upon that common error to flay the pretensions of mercantilism, as if the error could not just as readily flow from the doctrine of laissez-faire. He uttered an encomium to the press as the instrument through which the ideas of the leading elements of society enlightened the people and rendered them worthy to rule, and he concluded with a remark that no one seems to have flung back in his face when he announced the impregnability of King Cotton in 1858: "It is not Commerce that is King, nor Manufactures, nor Cotton, nor any single Art or Science, any more than those who wear the baubles-crowns. Knowledge is Sovereign, and the Press is the royal seat on which she sits, a sceptered Monarch."[41]

Thus, after excoriating the despised bourgeoisie that delivered the bloodless blows fatal to chivalry and social order, and after condemning the visionary theorists of the Enlightenment who ushered in the horrors of the French Revolution and the rejection of Christian morality, Hammond ended with a paean to "knowledge." Although he carefully warned against the identification of knowledge solely with the methods of modern science and insisted upon the continuing claims of classical learning and Christian revelation, his audience might be forgiven for thinking that was singing the praises of the devil's own work. For he defended classical learning and Christian revelation primarily as contributions, not alternatives, to modern thought. The knowledge he enthroned in place of commerce, manufactures, and cotton remained the very scientific knowledge that had produced the new man of the post-French revolutionary era — that very new man against whose works he had been protesting throughout his life.

Hammond's intellectual ambiguity exposed the emotional ambivalence with which he faced the modern world. For whatever his personal weaknesses, and however much they may account for his political paralysis in the 1850s, his long quarrel with himself over the nature and meaning of the nineteenth century eerily reflected the dilemma of his class in its effort to build a modern slave society. Hammond had plenty of company in feeling torn over his attitude toward "progress" and where it was coming out in the nineteenth century, but few of his peers matched his insight into the attendant political dilemma of the South. As governor of South Carolina, Hammond ranked as a progressive. He brought in Edmund Ruffin, the noted soil chemist and exponent of scientific agriculture, to conduct an agricultural survey and to recommend reforms that could arrest the economic decline of the state. He tried to persuade a conservative legislature to make substantial appropriations to expand education, at least for the middle classes. He identified himself with calls for industrial and commercial development. The office of governor had little power in such matters beyond that of exhortation, but he did the little he could. That he failed to accomplish much constitutes no point against him. The legislature did business as usual, and even if it had responded more vigorously, the structural impediments that slave society imposed would have compromised the effort from the start.

Hammond had begun his career as a militant nullifier and during the 1840s had remained on the far right of Calhoun's coalition, when he was not sniping at it from without. By his own later admission he had favored the secession of South Carolina in those days and even in the late 1840s. He and his good friend William Gilmore Simms exchanged letters in which they came close to expressing the hope that an allegedly indecisive Calhoun would die and get out of the way. Yet Hammond wavered during the struggle over the Compromise of 1850, just when Calhoun finally threw down the gauntlet to the North, and he hurt his chances by an erratic course at the Nashville Convention. When, during the late 1850s, South Carolina finally forgave or at least decided to overlook his sins and sent him to the United States Senate — when South Carolina was at last moving toward the resolute action he had once advocated — he disappointed his supporters by opposing secession. He explained himself in October 1858, in a defensive and wavering speech at Barnwell Court House. He gave every indication of having lost his nerve and may well have finished himself politically.[42]

Hammond had no faith in South Carolina's ability to win the war on which it was embarking. By the 1850s, he seems to have had no faith that even a united South could win a war with the North. Calling upon South Carolina to eschew secession, he appears to have doubted that the South could survive outside the Union he detested. He repeated some of the brave old words about southern rights and his willingness to fight to the death, but the fire was gone. It had been doused not only by the cumulative effect of personal woes and disappointments, but by the cold analysis that had emerged from years of study and brooding in the political wilderness. For no matter how much Hammond criticized the emerging world of science and industry and enlisted the wisdom of the ancients and the eternal truths of Christianity to encourage skepticism about the reality of moral progress and enlightenment, he understood too well that the genie was out of the bottle—that science and industry had created a self-revolutionizing world in which the relation of political and military forces had shifted decisively to the despised bourgeoisie.

In his letters to Clarkson, in his address at South Carolina College, and on other occasions on which he discussed progress, Hammond sounded like a philosophical idealist. He displayed his eloquence contrapuntally, first in his vivid descriptions of the wonders of scientific and material developments, and then in his ringing calls for a spiritual backfire against their pernicious effects. Yet a curiously materialist bias kept breaking through his rhetoric. Time and again, when political decisiveness alone might have realized his calls for that backfire, he found the timing wrong. The South, including South Carolina, was not ready for combat. It was backward in too many essential respects, and on close inspection those respects turn out to have been overwhelmingly economic.

Hammond displayed an extraordinary penchant for falling back on essentially economic-determinist arguments against bold action by the South, much as he let economic-determinist assumptions lead him into the dangerous nonsense that the North would not dare to make war on cotton. It were as if, foreshadowing the arguments of Plekhanov and the Mensheviks of 1917, not to mention those of some timid Bolsheviks, he was ready to stand for revolution only until a Lenin came along with April Theses to proclaim that politics commanded economics and that the time had come to act boldly. One of the most dismal moments in Hammond's speech at Barnwell Court House came with the assurance that abolitionism was waning in front of economic realities. The northern bourgeoisie, it seems, knew that the antislavery agitation was bad for business and would soon put the abolitionists down.[43]

An appeal to the businessmen of the North to consult their own pecuniary interests echoed an old theme from the debates over slavery in the Federal Constitutional Convention, where the northerners appeared to have yielded to southern taunts to consider their own pecuniary interests.[44] No wonder, then, that many southern unionists reacted with surprise when northerners voted for the Republicans in apparent disregard of the profit motive that was supposed to spur their every action. An assumption that dollars and cents would ultimately determine the course of the North had become common fare in the South. During the 1840s and 1850s it became ever more widespread. No doubt some trumpeted it largely as a way to bully opponents and keep up their own spirits, but, for most, it flowed inexorably from the prevailing view of bourgeois society in general and of the northern in particular. Southrons, it seems, rallied to honor, Yankees to money.

During the 1840s unionists like Henry St. George Tucker and southern nationalists like William Gilmore Simms agreed on the probable political effects of the stake of northern business in the southern economy. That stake, Tucker assured his law students at the University of Virginia, provided an insurmountable bulwark against abolitionist agitation. Simms believed that northern capitalists, as well as farmers and laborers, opposed slavery and could not be trusted. "Force them to take sides," he wrote Hammond in 1847, "& they side against us to a man, however reluctantly." Yet he wrote Calhoun only a few months earlier, "I think the popular greed will put down the abolitionist faction at the North, if once satisfied that the acquisition of territory cannot be made unless the South is pacified."[45]

From the crisis of 1850 to that of 1860, radicals and moderates alike played variations on the theme, urging nonintercourse with the North as a way of pressuring northern business to take sterner measures against the abolitionists or, if things went badly, to let the South secede peacefully. "Would the manufacturing States wish to risk a war," Nathaniel Beverley Tucker rhetorically asked the Nashville Convention, "which, while it lasted, would shut them out of the best market in the world?" Theorists like George Fitzhugh and politicians like Governor John Pettus of Mississippi preached nonintercourse with increasing fervor, expressing confidence in its salutary political results. Combining a variety of delusions, Pettus crowed in 1860 that nonintercourse would "turn New England upside down in six months. Half her population would be paupers from the day the Southern States ceased to trade with her." Even the staunch unionist and politically sober Benjamin F. Perry of South Carolina had such flights of fancy, which others carried into the war years as "King Cotton Diplomacy." The strength of the "Cotton-Is-King" argument may be measured by the adherence to it of even the worldly-wise Trescot, who normally displayed an admirable grasp of international realities.[46]

Senator Stephen Mallory of Florida, subsequently the Confederacy's secretary of the navy, wrote Hammond that he too saw northern businessmen in retreat from the precipice: "[Their] brains are being reached through their bellies." During the 1840s and 1850s nonintercourse and a variety of less dramatic measures were advanced by those most concerned with the promotion of southern commerce and industry as the best way to defeat the abolitionists in the North. Even with the onset of secession, prominent men like T. R. R. Cobb clung to the hope that the businessmen of the North, facing an economic debacle, would force reunion on a basis acceptable to the South.[47]

The economic argument had its critics. Alfred A. Smith of South Carolina, among others, accepted the "Cotton-Is-King" argument but concluded, as Beverley Tucker had done years before, that it made the South safe for secession by deterring the North from war. Smith denied that "the people of the North are awakening to a just perception of our rights." Senator Albert Iverson of Georgia directly criticized Hammond's claim that abolitionism was receding in the North: "In my opinion, there never was a greater mistake." Those who know human nature, he insisted in a particularly unkind cut, must know that antislavery fanaticism will never yield to economic interests and will not settle for less than the final abolition of slavery. Hammond, who prided himself on his insights into the human psyche, must have winced at the thrust. And Hammond surely had to recognize himself as an object of the attack leveled by Thomas Walton of Mississippi against Leonidas Spratt, the South's leading exponent of the reopening of the African slave trade. Walton chided Spratt for assuming that the North operated on pocketbook considerations alone and would therefore yield to southern demands. A unionist, Walton warned that Spratt failed to grasp the psychological dimension of the sectional struggle and, in particular, gravely underestimated the danger of a northern fanaticism that could only spread in the wake of reckless southern demands.[48]

"Python," a frequent contributor to *DeBow's Review* and hailed by DeBow himself as "brilliant," offered a more conspiratorial theory in reply to the argument of Senator R. M. T. Hunter of Virginia and, by extension, to that of Hammond. He agreed that the prosperity of the North depended upon black southern labor, but he argued that the wily northern capitalists and politicians intended to destroy the planter class and patriarchal slavery in order to replace them with northern capitalists and a viciously exploitative disguised slavery that would compel blacks to work for bare subsistence without any protection against unemployment or support during illness, infirmity, and old age. "The North," he wrote, "have no insane idea of destroying the negro labor, or of losing the precious products of that labor. They only mean that the negroes shall work directly for themselves instead of indirectly as now."[49]

Privately, Hammond expressed his own doubts. He believed that England and France would collapse without southern cotton, but he worried about the northern reaction to an economic confrontation. In a retrospective entry in his "secret diary" in April 1861, he wrote that he had not feared the abolitionists so much as the North's "corrupt and ignorant Politicians, and its Capitalists, who have built up and would continue to sustain its Commerce, its Manufactures, its whole Mercantile and Financial System *at our Cost*, and in the Union *in despite of us*."[50] Hammond thus reversed the point he had made at Barnwell Court House. Perhaps he was simply indulging in a self-serving lapse of memory. More likely he never did believe the northern business interests would put down the abolitionists and had been desperately reaching for arguments to stem a secessionist tide that was leading the South into a debacle.

The South, then, had to contain the threat of a militant northern response to the threat of secession while it forged itself into a modern nation by matching the material performance of the North. If the South seceded prematurely, it would not be able to sustain itself. It would need years to develop its infrastructure, reclaim its worn-out soils, and educate its people. It would need years of conscious effort, unprecedented social discipline, and strong leadership. Hammond had come a long way since the mid 1830s, when, writing to Beverley Tucker, he had boldly predicted secession and the South's emergence as the most prosperous country in history.[51]

Yet Hammond made no effort to anticipate the obvious objection: During those years of projected southern development would not the North forge even farther ahead? Could slavery, for all its alleged superiority as a social system, match, much less surpass, the performance of industrial capitalism? And if not, would not the South have to resort to some form of industrial capitalism and thereby replicate all the evils Hammond had long and fiercely condemned?

Implicitly, Hammond had an answer, which many proslavery Unionists periodically advanced: The impending social crisis of free societies, rooted in the deepening class struggle between capital and labor, would compel them to institute some form of slavery and thereby end their hostility to the South. Hence, it made sense for the South to play a waiting game. But this plea faltered. Most unionists agreed with Dew that uncultivated land and unique economic conditions would allow the North to escape a confrontation with its own social question for a long time to come. Suppose those greedy and selfish capitalists could not or would not stem the rising tide of antislavery radicalism in a North hell-bent for economic development and sure of its own superior virtue?

Hammond could not wholly believe his own scenarios, and, as he grew older, he displayed a deepening fear of plunges into the unknown. Those rhetorical flourishes in which he could not keep from extolling the very material progress he would proceed to criticize and denounce betrayed a deep longing for the forbidden fruit of the bourgeois world and a horrified sense that, like it or not, the bourgeoisie's march to world power could not be arrested. At the world-weary age of forty-eight he lamented, "If I live and prosper I will improve the place, *Lay* my bones there, and leave it for a family mansion. But I am now too old, too infirm, too heart broken to do anything with spirit or look forward to any earthly enjoyments."[52]

Hammond died during the war a spiritually broken man. As Drew Faust has suggested in her excellent biography, the horrors of the War — the mass slaughter made possible by a rapidly developing and terrible technology as well as by an astonishing callousness toward human life — deepened Hammond's sense that "progress" was out of control. Apparently, he saw no way to stop it and, given his lifelong ambivalence toward its fruits, he could only surrender to a fear that his preferred society, as well as he himself, had no future. Shortly before he died, although only in his mid fifties, he told his son that he had lived too long. In his heart he felt the paralyzing truth: His beloved southern slave society had also lived too long.

NOTES

1. William Henry Trescot, *The Diplomacy of the Revolution: An Historical Study* (New York: D. Appleton, 1852), p. 5. See also Trescot, *The Diplomatic History of the Administrations of Washington and Adams, 1789–1801* (Boston: Little, Brown, 1857), which develops the main themes. On Trescot see David Moltke-Hansen's fine if all-too-brief study, "William Henry Trescot," *Dictionary of Literary Biography*, vol. 30, pp. 310–319; and "A Beaufort Planter's Rhetorical World: The Contexts and Contents of William Henry Trescot's Orations," *Proceedings of the South Carolina Historical Association* (1981), 120–132; also Robert Nicholas Olsberg, "A Government of Class and Race: William Henry Trescot and the South Carolina Chivalry, 1860–1865" (Ph.D. diss., University of South Carolina, 1972).

2. Trescot, *Diplomacy of the Revolution*, p. 148; also pp. 141–142.

3. Trescot, *Diplomacy of the Revolution*, pp. 151–152. The merits of Trescot's ultraconservative interpretation of the American Revolution need not detain us, but for a much different view from a recent conservative scholar see Thomas L. Pangle, *The Spirit of Modern Republicanism: The Moral Vision of the American Founders and the Philosophy of Locke* (Chicago: University of Chicago Press, 1988), esp. p. 278.

4. Condemnation of the French as a people unfit for freedom became widespread in the South during the nineteenth century. More to the point, it increasingly appeared in a context that subdivided Europeans into quasi-racial groups. As the celebration of Caucasian peoples advanced, so did a pronounced tendency to distinguish among ostensibly superior and inferior Caucasians in a manner that sometimes suggested more than historical and cultural differences. Needless to say, the Anglo-Saxons, Teutons, and some Celts were granted pride of place.

5. Olsberg, "Government of Class and Race," pp. 120–124, 179–180; the direct quotation is from p. 120.

6. Trescot to Thornwell, June 25, 1856, in the Thornwell Papers at the University of South Carolina.

7. Trescot to Miles, Feb. 8, 1859, cited in Olsberg, "Government of Class and Race," pp. 122–123.

8. Moltke-Hansen, "William Henry Trescot," *Dictionary of Literary Biography*, vol. 30, p. 318.

9. Trescot, *The Position and Course of the South* (Charleston: Walker & James, 1850).

10. Trescot, *Position and Course*, p. 10.

11. Olsberg, "Government of Class and Race," pp. 79–80. In addition to Trescot's *Position and Course*, see his "The Future of Our Confederation," *DeBow's Review*, 6 (1859), 289–297; and *Annual Address before the Calleiopean and Polytechnic Societies of the Citadel* (Charleston: Walker & Evans, 1856).

12. Trescot, *Position and Course*, p. 10; subsequent quotations from pp. 10–11. Trescot doubted that the racially superior whites could be held in slavery, but he nonetheless projected slavery as the model for a future world order. In short, he seems to have recoiled from the logic of his own argument and to have tried to keep the options open. See Trescot, "South Carolina – A Colony and State," *DeBow's Review*, 27 (Dec. 1859), 685–687.

13. Trescot, *An American View of the Eastern Question* (Charleston: John Russell, 1854), pp. 14, 58.

14. In 1870, Trescot rewrote his own history, dissociating himself from those extremists who had departed from racial and constitutional arguments and unwisely advocated slavery on principle. He was by no means alone – Andrew Johnson provides an especially amusing example – in forgetting that he had himself done precisely that before the War. See Trescot, *Memorial of the Life of J. Johnston Pettigrew, Brig. Gen. of the Confederate States Army* (Charleston: John Russell, 1870), p. 36.

15. Historians have long noticed that the unionists of the plantation states, and many of the yeoman areas of the border states as well, were emphatically proslavery. But they were more than that. A large number, including – of all people – Parson Brownlow and Andrew Johnson, openly supported the theory of "slavery in the abstract," which held that some form of slavery was the inevitable condition of the laboring classes regardless of race. Brownlow could hardly have been clearer in his debate with the abolitionist Rev. A. Prynne. Johnson forcefully associated himself with Hammond on this point in his reply in the Senate to the "Cotton Is King" speech, in which he merely elaborated on a view he had long been espousing. See William G. Brownlow and A. Prynne, *Ought American Slavery to Be Perpetuated?: A Debate between Rev. W. G. Brownlow and Rev. A. Prynne Held at Philadelphia, September, 1858* (Miami, Fla.: Mnemosyne Publishing Co., 1969 [1858]); Leroy P. Graf, Ralph W. Haskins, and Paul H. Bergeron, eds., *The Papers of Andrew Johnson* (8 vols. to date; Knoxville, Tenn.: University of Tennessee Press, 1967–), III, 158–160.

16. On Hammond, see esp. Drew Gilpin Faust's admirable study, *James Henry Hammond and the Old South: A Design for Mastery* (Baton Rouge: Louisiana State University Press, 1982). Faust relates Hammond to other leading figures in *A Sacred Circle: The Dilemma of the Intellectual in the Old South, 1840–1860* (Baltimore: Johns Hopkins University Press, 1977). See also Robert Cinnamond Tucker, "James Henry Hammond: South Carolinian" (Ph.D. diss., University of North Carolina, 1958). Carol Bleser and Clyde N. Wilson have offered excellent insights into the man and his times and thought in their editions of Hammond's private papers and writings. See Bleser, ed., *The Hammonds of Redcliffe* (New York: Oxford University Press, 1981), and *Secret and Sacred: The Diaries of James Henry Hammond, a Southern Slaveholder* (New York: Oxford University Press, 1988); and Wilson's introduction to the reprint edition of James H. Hammond, *Selections from the Letters and Speeches of the Hon. James H. Hammond* (Spartanburg, S. C.: The Reprint Co., 1978 [1866]), pp. xi–xxv. There are useful remarks scattered in Fred Hobson, *Tell about the South: The Southern Rage to Explain* (Baton Rouge:

Louisiana State University Press, 1983). Especially valuable on Hammond's political course are Charles M. Wiltse, *John C. Calhoun* (3 vols.; Indianapolis: Bobbs-Merrill, 1944–1951); and W. W. Freehling, *Road to Disunion*. Still useful for particular points are Elizabeth Merritt, *James Henry Hammond, 1807–1864* (Baltimore: Johns Hopkins University Press, 1923); and Clement Eaton, *The Mind of the Old South* (Baton Rouge: Louisiana State University Press, 1964), pp. 21–42.

There is a special problem for those who would interpret Hammond. Carol Bleser has forcefully reminded me that, however much one may wish to give him the benefit of the doubt, he comes through his own personal papers as having had an unusually high quotient of hypocrisy. In politics as well as in his personal life he was capable of saying almost anything if it suited his purposes. Consequently, one must take special pains with the materials he committed to print. I nonetheless insist that he carried through his principal themes with surprising consistency, notwithstanding the shifts in his political judgments. I know of nothing in his personal papers to suggest that he did not firmly adhere to the social philosophy he expressed in his public utterances, and his severest critics have not charged him on that account.

17. Hammond, *Letters and Speeches*, pp. 15–50; quote from p. 45.

18. Ibid., pp. 41–42; quote from p. 41.

19. Ibid., pp. 43–44.

20. Ibid., pp. 44–45.

21. Quoted by Bleser, *Hammonds of Redcliffe*, p. 7.

22. See esp. Faust's analysis of Hammond's views in *James Henry Hammond*, ch. 10.

23. Hammond, *Letters and Speeches*, pp. 105–113, esp. pp. 108–110.

24. Ibid., p. 103.

25. Ibid., pp. 119–120.

26. Ibid., p. 128. Drew Faust, in her biography and in private communication, has suggested a more generous way to read Hammond on this matter. As his references to "human society" indicate, in the manner of Calhoun, he distinguished sharply between the "real world" of human beings as participants in society and the philosophical "abstraction" of human beings, which would reduce them to autonomous atoms. He clearly scoffed at any idea of human perfectibility, in any of its meanings, and acknowledged human depravity, even if he remained suspicious of the theological accounts of its origins. Under the circumstances, he may have meant to do no more than indicate that slavery was a divinely and historically sanctioned form of an inevitable social stratification that could take a variety of forms. But if such was his meaning, he was saying no more or less than the advocates of "slavery in the abstract" themselves were saying.

27. Ibid., pp. 153–154, 185.

28. Ibid., p. 159.

29. Ibid., pp. 317–318.

30. Ibid., p. 318.

31. Wilson, Introduction to Hammond, *Letters and Speeches*, p. xxiii.

32. See, e.g., "Speech at Barnwell Court House, Oct. 29, 1858," in Ham-

mond, *Letters and Speeches*, p. 338. Hammond prepared his Mudsill speech with great care as a reply to Seward, with whom he had an unusual personal exchange. Seward told him he believed the Union stronger than abolition in the North and slavery in the South. Hammond replied that Seward was half right — right about the North, wrong about the South. In any case, Hammond complimented himself on the speech: "It justified my friends and my State in sending me there. It fixed me at once as the Peer of any man on the Senate floor." Hammond Diary, April 16, 1861, Bleser, ed., *Secret and Sacred*, pp. 273–274. Still, while he assured himself that the "rank and file" of the South applauded his effort, he noted a cold reception from the politicians, many of whom may well have preferred a more restrained tone and content. See J. H. Hammond to M. C. M. Hammond, March 9, 1858, in Bleser, ed., *Hammonds of Redcliffe*, p. 42.

33. Hammond, *Letters and Speeches*, pp. 170–171.

34. Ibid., p. 171.

35. Ibid., p. 199. For an illuminating analysis on the attempt to rescue Bacon from the Utilitarians see Faust, *Sacred Circle*, pp. 71–73.

36. W. Hooper to J. T. Thornwell, April 11, 1850, in the Thornwell Papers at the Southern Historical Collection of the University of North Carolina.

37. Weaver, *Ideas Have Consequences* (Chicago: University of Chicago Press, 1948), p. 38.

38. J. B. Bury, *The Idea of Progress: An Inquiry into Its Origin and Growth* (New York: Dover, 1958), pp. 210–211.

39. Hammond, *Letters and Speeches*, p. 211.

40. Ibid., pp. 210–213; quote from pp. 212–213.

41. Ibid., p. 228.

42. The lingering response to Hammond's escapades may be gleaned from the outburst of William Campbell Preston, one of the leading lights of the Establishment in South Carolina and a man who found Hammond's politics as distasteful as his morals. "What a sin and disgrace," he wrote Waddy Thompson in 1857, "it will be to elect Hammond Senator — a knave and a scoundrel. How much better to take *Pickens* who has it may be foibles but not crimes — Orr is the man and he ought to be forced to take it." Preston to Thompson, July 22, 1857, in the Preston Papers at the University of South Carolina.

Hammond initially fretted over the impact of his speech at Barnwell Court House. In November 1855 he whined about the rough treatment he received from the "spies called reporters" and pronounced the speech "too full of truth for present digestion," advising William Porcher Miles to "lie low about it." Two months later he wrote Simms that the speech scored a great success. See Hammond to Miles, Nov. 5, 1858, in the Miles Papers; Hammond to Simms, Jan. 1, 1859, in Simms, *Letters*, IV, 102, n. 2.

43. Hammond, *Letters and Speeches*, p. 346.

44. Cathy D. Matson and Peter S. Onuf, *A Union of Interests: Political and Economic Thought in Revolutionary America* (Lawrence: University of Kansas Press, 1990), pp. 118–119; Clyde N. Wilson, *Carolina Cavalier: The Life and Mind of James Johnston Pettigrew* (Athens: University of Georgia Press, 1990), p. 112.

45. H. St. G. Tucker, *Lectures on Government*, pp. 180–185. Simms to Hammond, May 1, 1847; Simms to Calhoun, Feb. 10, 1847 – in Simms, *Letters*, II, 312, 267.

46. For Beverly Tucker's speech see *Southern Quarterly Review*, 18 (1850), 218; for Pettus see Arthur C. Cole, *The Irrepressible Conflict, 1850–1865* (New York: Macmillan, 1934), p. 67; B. F. Perry, speech in the S. C. House of Representatives, Dec. 11, 1850, in Stephen Meats and Edwin T. Arnold, eds., *The Writings of Benjamin F. Perry* (3 vols.; Spartanburg, S. C.: The Reprint Co., 1980), I, 367–368; Trescot, "Our Commission to Europe – What Are the Facts?" *DeBow's Review*, 31 (1861), 412–419. In general see Frank Lawrence Owsley, *King Cotton Diplomacy: Foreign Relations of the Confederate States of America* (2nd ed., rev. by Harriet Chappel Owsley; Chicago: University of Chicago Press, 1959).

47. Mallory quoted in Joseph T. Durkin, *Stephen R. Mallory, Confederate Navy Chief* (Chapel Hill: University of North Carolina Press, 1954), p. 119; Pratt, letter quoted in *DeBow's Review*, 10 (1851), 227; G. F. H. Tarrant, ed., *Hon. Daniel Pratt, A Biography* (Richmond, Va., 1904), pp. 75–76; James Martin, *DeBow's Review*, 24 (1858), 382; William Gregg, *DeBow's Review*, 30 (1860); 77; Fletcher M. Green, "Duff Green: Industrial Promoter," *Journal of Southern History*, 2 (1936), 29–30; E. Steadman and James Robb, in J. D. B. DeBow, ed., *The Industrial Resources of the Southern and Western States* (3 vols.; New York: Appleton, 1854), II, 127, 154. For similar views expressed at commercial conventions see Weymouth T. Jordan, *Ante-Bellum Alabama* (Tallahassee: Florida State University Press, 1957), pp. 141–142; and esp. Herbert Wender, *Southern Commercial Conventions, 1837–1859* (Baltimore: Johns Hopkins University Press, 1930), pp. 9–10, 188, 193, 195. Wender writes (p. 193): "According to Mr. W. W. Boyce, of South Carolina, the destinies of England and of the North were hanging upon a thread of cotton."

48. Alfred A. Smith, "A Southern Confederacy: Its Prospect, Resources, and Destiny," *DeBow's Review*, 26 (1859), 572; excerpt from the speech of Sen. Iverson of Georgia in "Editorial Miscellany," *DeBow's Review*, 26 (1859), 349; Thomas Walton, "Further Views of the Advocates of the Slave Trade," *DeBow's Review*, 26 (1859), 53.

49. Python, "The Secession of the South," *DeBow's Review*, 28 (1860), 387–388; quote from p. 388.

50. Hammond Diary, April 16, 1861; also Sept. 11, 1862 – in Bleser, ed., *Secret and Sacred*, pp. 278, 286.

51. Hammond to Tucker, March 11, 1836, quoted in James T. Carpenter, *The South as a Conscious Minority, 1789–1861: A Study in Political Thought* (New York: New York University Press, 1930), pp. 190–191.

52. Hammond Diary, May 12, 1855, Bleser, ed., *Hammonds of Redcliffe*, p. 19. Also, Bleser, ed., *Secret and Sacred*, pp. 266–267.

Index